WORSHIP the Only True God

To Our Readers

Everlasting life on a paradise earth! By means of a study of the Bible, we learn about this wonderful hope. But this, as well as other basic teachings of God's Word, is just a beginning. The Bible urges all who love God to "grasp mentally . . . [the] height and depth" of his precious truths. (Ephesians 3:18) To that end, this book has been prepared. We hope that it will help you to grow spiritually and to be better equipped to walk the narrow road leading to life in God's righteous new world.

—The Publishers

Publishers
WATCHTOWER BIBLE AND TRACT SOCIETY OF NEW YORK, INC.
INTERNATIONAL BIBLE STUDENTS ASSOCIATION
Brooklyn, New York, U.S.A.

First Printing in English: 5,000,000 Copies
Unless otherwise indicated, Scripture quotations
are from the modern-language
New World Translation of the Holy Scriptures—With References

Worship the Only True God
English (*wt*-E)
Made in the United States of America

Photo Credits: ▪ Cover: U.S. Navy photo ▪ Page 180: Children: UNITED NATIONS/J. FRANK

CONTENTS

'The meek ones will
possess the earth and
find their exquisite
delight in the
abundance of peace'

CHAPTER ONE

Unity of Worship in Our Time —What Does It Mean?

AROUND the globe there is a thrilling movement toward unity of worship. It is bringing together millions of people of all nations, tribes, and languages. More are being gathered each year. These are identified in the Bible as "witnesses" of Jehovah and are called "a great crowd." They render God "sacred service day and night." (Isaiah 43:10-12; Revelation 7:9-15) Why do they do this? Because they have come to know Jehovah as the only true God. This motivates them to bring their lives into harmony with his righteous ways. Also, they have learned that we are living in "the last days" of this present wicked world, that God will soon destroy it, and that he will replace it with his paradisaic new world.—2 Timothy 3:1-5, 13; 2 Peter 3:10-13.

2 God's Word promises: "Just a little while longer, and the wicked one will be no more . . . But the meek ones themselves will possess the earth, and they will indeed find their exquisite delight in the abundance of peace." (Psalm 37:10, 11) "The righteous themselves will possess the earth, and they will reside forever upon it." (Psalm 37:29) "[God] will wipe out every tear from their eyes, and death will be no more, neither will

---

1, 2. (a) What thrilling movement is taking place in our time? (b) What marvelous hope do honesthearted people have?

mourning nor outcry nor pain be anymore. The former things have passed away."—Revelation 21:4.

3 Those who are now being unified in true worship make up the first residents of that new world. They have learned what God's will is and are doing it to the best of their ability. Showing the importance of this, Jesus said: "This means everlasting life, their taking in knowledge of you, the only true God, and of the one whom you sent forth, Jesus Christ." (John 17:3) The apostle John wrote: "The world is passing away and so is its desire, but he that does the will of God remains forever."—1 John 2:17.

What It Really Means

4 What does the gathering of so many to united worship in our time really mean? It is clear evidence that we are very near to the end of this wicked world, with God's new world to begin right after that. We are eyewitnesses of the fulfillment of Bible prophecies that foretold this momentous ingathering. One such prophecy states: "It must occur in the final part of the days [these last days] that the mountain of the house of Jehovah [his elevated true worship] will become firmly established above the top of the mountains [above any other type of worship], . . . and to it peoples must stream. And many nations will certainly go and say: 'Come, you people, and let us go up to the mountain of Jehovah and to the house of the God of

---

3. How is true unity of worship being brought about?
4. (a) What does the gathering of so many in united worship in our time really mean? (b) How does the Bible describe this ingathering?

Jacob; and he will instruct us about his ways, and we will walk in his paths.'"—Micah 4:1, 2; Psalm 37:34.

5 While entire nations are not presenting themselves at Jehovah's spiritual house for worship, millions of individuals out of all nations are doing so. As they learn about the loving purpose and the appealing personality of Jehovah God, their hearts are deeply moved. They humbly seek to find out what God requires of them. Their prayer is like that of the psalmist who said: "Teach me to do your will, for you are my God."—Psalm 143:10.

6 Do you see yourself among the great crowd of people whom Jehovah is now bringing together in unified worship? Does your response to the instruction you have received from his Word show that you truly appreciate that Jehovah is its Source? To what extent will you "walk in his paths"?

How It Is Achieved

7 Jehovah's purpose is for all intelligent creation to be united in true worship. How we long for the day when all who live will worship the only true God! (Psalm 103:19-22) But before that can be, Jehovah must eliminate all who refuse to do his righteous will. Mercifully, he gives advance notice of what he will do, so that people everywhere can have the opportunity to change their course. (Isaiah 55:6, 7) Thus, in our day "to every

---

5, 6. (a) How is it true that nations are turning to Jehovah? (b) What questions should we ask ourselves?

7. (a) To what extent will unity of worship eventually be achieved? (b) Why is it urgent to become a worshiper of Jehovah now, and how can we help others to do that?

nation and tribe and tongue and people," this urgent appeal is being made: "Fear God and give him glory, because the hour of the judgment by him has arrived, and so worship the One who made the heaven and the earth and sea and fountains of waters." (Revelation 14: 6, 7) Have you accepted that invitation? If so, it is your privilege to invite yet others to know and worship the true God.

8 It is not Jehovah's purpose to be worshiped by people who say that they believe in him but who then continue to pursue their own interests. God wants people to come to an "accurate knowledge of his will" and reflect this in their lives. (Colossians 1:9, 10) Thus, appreciative people who learn the basic teachings of the Bible want to press on to Christian maturity. Their desire is to get to know Jehovah more intimately, to broaden and deepen their understanding of his Word, and to apply it more fully in their lives. They seek to reflect the qualities of our heavenly Father and to view matters as he does. This moves them to search out ways to share in the lifesaving work that he is having done in the earth in our day. Is that also your desire? —Mark 13:10; Hebrews 5:12–6:3.

9 The Bible shows that those who serve Jehovah must be a united people. (Ephesians 4:1-3) This unity is to exist now, even though we live in a divided world and are still struggling with our own imperfections. Jesus earnestly prayed that all his disciples be one, enjoy-

---

8. After learning basic Bible teachings, what further progress should we earnestly endeavor to make?
9. In what ways is true unity possible now?

ing true unity. What would this mean? First, that they would have a good relationship with Jehovah and his Son. Second, that they would be united with one another. (John 17:20, 21) To that end, the Christian congregation serves as the organization through which Jehovah instructs his people.

What Factors Contribute to Unity?

10 Seven key factors that contribute to unity of worship are noted below. As you answer the accompanying questions, give thought to how each point affects your relationship with Jehovah and with fellow Christians. Reasoning on these points and looking up the scriptures cited but not quoted will contribute to your development of godly wisdom, thinking ability, and discernment—qualities all of us need. (Proverbs 5:1, 2; Philippians 1:9-11) Consider these factors one at a time.

(1) ***We acknowledge Jehovah's right to set the standard as to good and bad.*** "Trust in Jehovah with all your heart and do not lean upon your own understanding. In all your ways take notice of him, and he himself will make your paths straight."—Proverbs 3:5, 6.

Why should we seek Jehovah's counsel and guidance when making decisions? (Psalm 146:3-5; Isaiah 48:17)

(2) ***We have God's Word to guide us.*** "When you received God's word, which you heard from us, you

---

10. (a) What do we develop when we personally use the Bible to reason out answers to questions that affect us? (b) Analyze the factors contributing to Christian unity by answering the questions listed in this paragraph.

accepted it, not as the word of men, but, just as it truthfully is, as the word of God, which is also at work in you believers."—1 Thessalonians 2:13.

What danger is there in simply doing what we "feel" is right? (Proverbs 14:12; Jeremiah 10:23, 24; 17:9)

If we do not know what counsel the Bible gives on a certain matter, what should we do? (Proverbs 2: 3-5; 2 Timothy 3:16, 17)

(3) *We all benefit from the same spiritual feeding program.* "All your sons will be persons taught by Jehovah." (Isaiah 54:13) "Let us consider one another to incite to love and fine works, not forsaking the gathering of ourselves together, as some have the custom, but encouraging one another, and all the more so as you behold the day [of destruction] drawing near." —Hebrews 10:24, 25.

What benefits come to those who take full advantage of Jehovah's arrangements for spiritual feeding? (Isaiah 65:13, 14)

(4) *Jesus Christ, and no human, is our Leader.* "Do not you be called Rabbi, for one is your teacher, whereas all you are brothers. Moreover, do not call anyone your father on earth, for one is your Father, the heavenly One. Neither be called 'leaders,' for your Leader is one, the Christ."—Matthew 23:8-10.

Should any of us believe that we are superior to others? (Romans 3:23, 24; 12:3)

(5) *We look to God's Kingdom government as the only hope for humankind.* "You must pray, then, this way:

'Our Father in the heavens, let your name be sanctified. Let your kingdom come. Let your will take place, as in heaven, also upon earth.' Keep on, then, seeking first the kingdom and his righteousness."—Matthew 6:9, 10, 33.

How does "seeking first the kingdom" help safeguard our unity? (Micah 4:3; 1 John 3:10-12)

(6) ***Holy spirit produces in worshipers of Jehovah qualities that are vital to Christian unity.*** "The fruitage of the spirit is love, joy, peace, long-suffering, kindness, goodness, faith, mildness, self-control."—Galatians 5: 22, 23.

What must we do in order for God's spirit to produce its fruitage in us? (Acts 5:32)

How does having God's spirit influence our relationship with fellow Christians? (John 13:35; 1 John 4:8, 20, 21)

(7) ***All of God's true worshipers share in preaching the good news of his Kingdom.*** "This good news of the kingdom will be preached in all the inhabited earth for a witness to all the nations; and then the end will come."—Matthew 24:14.

What should motivate us to want to have a full share in this preaching activity? (Matthew 22:37-39; Romans 10:10)

11 Unitedly worshiping Jehovah draws us closer to him and enables us to enjoy refreshing association with fellow believers. Psalm 133:1 says: "Look! How

---

11. When we apply Bible truths in our lives, what is the effect?

good and how pleasant it is for brothers to dwell together in unity!" How refreshing it is to get away from the world with all its selfishness, immorality, and violence and to congregate with those who truly love Jehovah and obey his laws!

Avoid Divisive Influences

12 So as not to mar our precious global unity, we must avoid divisive influences. One of these is the spirit of independence from God and his laws. Jehovah helps us to avoid it by unmasking its originator, Satan the Devil. (2 Corinthians 4:4; Revelation 12:9) Satan is the one who influenced Adam and Eve to ignore what God had said and to make decisions contrary to God's will. The result was calamity for them and for us. (Genesis 3:1-6, 17-19) This world is saturated with the spirit of independence from God and his laws. So we need to curb that spirit in ourselves.

13 For example, consider Jehovah's thrilling promise to replace the present wicked world with new heavens and a new earth in which "righteousness is to dwell." (2 Peter 3:13) Should that not move us to begin preparing to live at that time when righteousness will prevail? This means heeding the Bible's plain counsel: "Do not be loving either the world or the things in the world. If anyone loves the world, the love of the Father is not in him." (1 John 2:15) Hence, we shun this world's spirit—its independent attitude, its excessive concern for self, its immorality and violence. We make

---

12. Why do we need to avoid an independent spirit?
13. What will show whether we are sincerely preparing for life in God's righteous new world?

it a practice to listen to Jehovah and to obey him from our heart, despite any contrary inclinations of the imperfect flesh. Our entire life course gives evidence that our thinking and our motives are oriented to doing God's will.—Psalm 40:8.

14 When the appointed time comes for Jehovah to destroy this wicked system of things and all who prefer its ways, he will not delay. He is not going to postpone that time or change his standards to accommodate those who are still trying to cling to the world while halfheartedly learning God's will and doing it. Now is the time for action! (Luke 13:23, 24; 17:32; 21:34-36) How heartwarming it is, therefore, to see the great crowd taking hold of this precious opportunity, eagerly seeking the instruction that Jehovah provides through his Word and organization and unitedly walking in his paths toward the new world! And the more we learn about Jehovah, the more we will love him and want to serve him.

---

14. (a) Why is it important to seize the opportunity now to learn Jehovah's ways and to follow them in our lives? (b) What do the scriptures cited in the paragraph mean to us personally?

Review Discussion

- What is Jehovah's purpose as to worship?
- After we have learned basic Bible teachings, what further progress should we earnestly seek to make?
- What can we individually do to be in unity with other worshipers of Jehovah?

Jehovah, in his
great love,
'will open his hand and
satisfy the desire
of every living thing'

CHAPTER TWO

Magnify Jehovah as the Only True God

THE Bible says that although there are many who are viewed as gods, "there is actually to us one God the Father." (1 Corinthians 8:5, 6) That "one God" is Jehovah, the Creator of all things. (Deuteronomy 6:4; Revelation 4:11) Jesus referred to him as "my God and your God." (John 20:17) He agreed with Moses, who had earlier stated: "Jehovah is the true God; there is no other besides him." (Deuteronomy 4:35) Jehovah is far superior to any objects of worship, such as idols, deified humans, or his enemy Satan the Devil, "the god of this system of things." (2 Corinthians 4:3, 4) In contrast to all of these, Jehovah is, as Jesus called him, "the *only* true God."—John 17:3.

2 Appreciative people who learn about God's heartwarming qualities, as well as what he has done and will yet do for us, are drawn to him. As their love for Jehovah grows, they feel impelled to magnify him. How? One way is by telling others about him. "With the mouth one makes public declaration for salvation," states Romans 10:10. Another way is by imitating him in word and deed. "Become imitators of God, as beloved children," says Ephesians 5:1. To do so more fully, we need to know Jehovah as he truly is.

---

1. Who is the only true God?
2. As we learn about God, how should our lives be affected?

3 Throughout the Bible, there are many statements that identify God's outstanding qualities. His four main attributes are wisdom, justice, power, and love. 'With him there is *wisdom.*' (Job 12:13) "All his ways are *justice.*" (Deuteronomy 32:4) He is "vigorous in *power.*" (Isaiah 40:26) "God is *love.*" (1 John 4:8) However, of God's four main qualities, which is the most outstanding, the one that more than any other identifies what kind of God he is?

"God Is Love"

4 Consider what motivated Jehovah to create the universe and intelligent spirit and human creatures. Was it his wisdom or power? No, for while God used those, they were not the motivating forces. And his justice did not require that he share the gift of life. Rather, God's great love prompted him to share the joys of intelligent existence with others. Love moved him to purpose that obedient mankind should live forever in Paradise. (Genesis 1:28; 2:15) Love caused him to arrange for the lifting of the condemnation that Adam's transgression brought upon mankind.

5 Thus, of all of God's qualities, the most outstanding is his love. It is his essence, or nature. As important as his wisdom, justice, and power are, the Bible never says that Jehovah *is* any of those. But it does say that he *is* love. Yes, Jehovah is the personification of love. This is love guided by principle, not emotion. God's

---

3. What are God's main qualities?
4. Which of God's qualities was fundamental to his creating the universe and all living things?
5. According to the Bible, Jehovah is the personification of which quality, and why?

love is governed by the principles of truth and righteousness. It is the highest form of love, as exemplified in Jehovah God himself. Such love is an expression of complete unselfishness and is always accompanied by tangible evidence of action.

6 It is this wonderful quality of love that enables us to imitate such a God. As lowly, imperfect, mistake-prone humans, we may think that we could never do so successfully. But here is another example of Jehovah's great love: He recognizes our limitations and does not require perfection of us. He knows that we are far from perfect now. (Psalm 51:5) That is why Psalm 130:3, 4 says: "If errors were what you watch, O Jah, O Jehovah, who could stand? For there is the true forgiveness with you." Yes, Jehovah is "a God merciful and gracious, slow to anger and abundant in loving-kindness." (Exodus 34:6) "You, O Jehovah, are good and ready to forgive." (Psalm 86:5) How comforting! How refreshing it is to serve this marvelous God and to experience his loving, merciful care!

7 Jehovah's love can also be seen in his works of creation. Think of the many good things Jehovah has provided for our enjoyment, such as beautiful mountains, forests, lakes, and oceans. He has given us food in amazing variety to delight our taste and sustain us. Too, Jehovah has provided a vast array of beautiful and fragrant flowers as well as the fascinating animal creation. He made things that would give humans

---

6. What makes it possible for us to imitate God, even though he is superior to us?
7. How can Jehovah's love be seen in his works of creation?

pleasure, even though he did not have to. True, living in this wicked world in our present imperfect condition, we cannot enjoy his creation to the full. (Romans 8:22) But just imagine what Jehovah will do for us in Paradise! The psalmist assures us: "You are opening your hand and satisfying the [proper] desire of every living thing."—Psalm 145:16.

8 What is the most outstanding example of Jehovah's love for humankind? The Bible explains: "God loved the world so much that he gave his only-begotten Son, in order that everyone exercising faith in him might not be destroyed but have everlasting life." (John 3:16) Was it because of man's goodness that Jehovah did this? Romans 5:8 answers: "God recommends his own love to us in that, while we were yet sinners, Christ died for us." Yes, God sent his perfect Son to earth to give his life as a ransom sacrifice to redeem us from the condemnation of sin and death. (Matthew 20:28) This opened the way for people who love God to gain everlasting life. Thankfully, God's love extends to all who want to do his will, for the Bible tells us: "God is not partial, but in every nation the man that fears him and works righteousness is acceptable to him."—Acts 10:34, 35.

9 How should the fact that Jehovah has given his Son as a ransom for us, opening the way to everlasting life, influence how we use our lives now? It should deepen

---

8. What is the most outstanding example of Jehovah's love for us?

9. How should we be influenced by the fact that Jehovah has given his Son as a ransom for us?

our love for the true God, Jehovah. At the same time, it should make us want to listen to Jesus, who represents God. "[Jesus] died for all that those who live might live no longer for themselves, but for him who died for them." (2 Corinthians 5:15) What a pleasure it is to follow in Jesus' footsteps, for he was exemplary in imitating Jehovah's love and compassion! This is shown by what Jesus said to humble ones: "Come to me, all you who are toiling and loaded down, and I will refresh you. Take my yoke upon you and learn from me, for I am mild-tempered and lowly in heart, and you will find refreshment for your souls. For my yoke is kindly and my load is light."—Matthew 11:28-30.

Showing Love for Others

10 How can we show that we have the kind of love for fellow Christians that Jehovah and Jesus have for us? Notice the many ways we can do this: "Love is long-suffering and kind. Love is not jealous, it does not brag, does not get puffed up, does not behave indecently, does not look for its own interests, does not become provoked. It does not keep account of the injury. It does not rejoice over unrighteousness, but rejoices with the truth. It bears all things, believes all things, hopes all things, endures all things. Love never fails." —1 Corinthians 13:4-8; 1 John 3:14-18; 4:7-12.

11 For whom else should we show love, and how? Jesus said: "Go therefore and make disciples of people of all the nations, baptizing them in the name of the Father and of the Son and of the holy spirit, teaching

---

10. What are some ways we can show love for fellow Christians?
11. For whom else should we show love, and how?

them to observe all the things I have commanded you." (Matthew 28:19, 20) This involves sharing the good news of God's incoming paradisaic new world with those who are not yet our fellow Christians. Jesus clearly showed that our love should not be limited to those sharing our beliefs, for he said: "If you love [only] those loving you, what reward do you have? Are not also the tax collectors doing the same thing? And if you greet your brothers only, what extraordinary thing are you doing? Are not also the people of the nations doing the same thing?"—Matthew 5:46, 47; 24: 14; Galatians 6:10.

"Walk in the Name of Jehovah"

12 Another important aspect of magnifying the true God is knowing, using, and teaching others his unique name, Jehovah. The psalmist expressed this heartfelt wish: "That people may know that you, whose name is Jehovah, you alone are the Most High over all the earth." (Psalm 83:18) The name Jehovah means "He Causes to Become." He is the Great Purposer, always bringing his purposes to a successful conclusion. And only the true God can rightly bear that name, for humans can never be sure that their efforts will succeed. (James 4:13, 14) Jehovah alone can say that his word "will have certain success" in that for which he sends it. (Isaiah 55:11) Many are thrilled when they first see God's name in their Bibles and learn what it means. (Exodus 6:3) But they will be benefited by this knowledge only if they "walk in the name of Jehovah . . . forever."—Micah 4:5.

---

12. Why can God's name apply only to him?

13 Regarding God's name, Psalm 9:10 states: "Those knowing your name will trust in you." This involves more than just knowing of the name Jehovah, which does not automatically mean trusting in him. Knowing God's name means appreciating the kind of God that Jehovah is, respecting his authority, obeying his commands, trusting him in all things. (Proverbs 3:5, 6) Similarly, walking in the name of Jehovah implies being dedicated to him and representing him as one of his worshipers, truly using our life in harmony with God's will. (Luke 10:27) Are you doing that?

14 If we are going to serve Jehovah eternally, more than a sense of duty must impel us. The apostle Paul urged Timothy, who had been serving Jehovah for many years: "Be training yourself with godly devotion as your aim." (1 Timothy 4:7) Devotion comes from a heart filled with appreciation for the person to whom the devotion is directed. "Godly devotion" expresses profound reverence for Jehovah personally. It manifests loving attachment to him because of unbounded esteem for him and his ways. It causes us to want everyone to hold his name in high regard. We must cultivate godly devotion in our lives if we would walk in the name of Jehovah, the only true God, forever. —Psalm 37:4; 2 Peter 3:11.

15 To serve God acceptably, we must give him undivided worship, since he is "a God exacting exclusive

---

13. What is involved in knowing Jehovah's name and walking in his name?
14. If we are going to serve Jehovah forever, what is needed besides a sense of duty?
15. How can we give God our exclusive devotion?

devotion." (Exodus 20:5) We cannot love God and at the same time love the wicked world, of which Satan is god. (James 4:4; 1 John 2:15-17) Jehovah knows exactly what kind of person each of us is trying to be. (Jeremiah 17:10) If we truly love righteousness, he sees that and will help us endure our daily trials. Backing us up with his powerful holy spirit, he will enable us to triumph over the wickedness so rampant in this world. (2 Corinthians 4:7) He will also help us maintain our strong hope of everlasting life on a paradise earth. What a glorious prospect that is! We should deeply appreciate it and willingly serve the true God, Jehovah, who makes it possible.

16 Millions of people earth wide have gladly accepted the invitation of the psalmist who wrote: "O magnify Jehovah with me, you people, and let us exalt his name together." (Psalm 34:3) Jehovah invites you to be among the growing multitudes in all nations who are doing this.

---

16. What should you want to do, along with millions of others?

Review Discussion

- What kind of person is Jehovah? How are we benefited by getting a clear understanding of his qualities?
- How can we help other people to learn the truth about God?
- What is involved in knowing Jehovah's name and walking in his name?

CHAPTER THREE

Keep a Firm Grip on the Word of God

"YOU well know with all your hearts and with all your souls that not one word out of all the good words that Jehovah your God has spoken to you has failed. They have all come true for you." (Joshua 23:14-16) This is what Joshua said to the older men of Israel after they were settled in the Promised Land. Yes, Jehovah's promises proved trustworthy. That record—and all the rest of the Bible—was preserved for us so that "we might have hope."—Romans 15:4.

2 Although some 40 human writers were used to record the Bible, Jehovah himself is its Author. Does this mean that he actively directed the writing of everything in it? Yes. He did this by means of his powerful holy spirit, his active force. The apostle Paul truthfully said: "All Scripture is inspired of God . . . that the man of God may be fully competent, completely equipped for every good work." People everywhere who are convinced of that pay heed to the Bible and build their lives around what it contains.—2 Timothy 3:16, 17; 1 Thessalonians 2:13.

---

1. (a) How did ancient Israel experience the truthfulness of God's word? (b) Why is that of interest to us?
2. (a) In what sense is the Bible "inspired of God"? (b) Knowing that the Bible is divinely inspired, what responsibility do we have?

Help Others to Appreciate It

3 Many to whom we speak do not share our conviction that the Bible is the Word of God. How can we help them? Often, the best way is to open the Bible and show them what it contains. "The word of God is alive and exerts power and is sharper than any two-edged sword . . . and is able to discern thoughts and intentions of the heart." (Hebrews 4:12) "The word of God" is not dead history; it is alive! The Bible's promises move irresistibly toward fulfillment. The influence of the Bible's message on a person's true heart motivation is more powerful than anything that we might personally say.

4 Seeing God's name there has caused many to peer deeper into the Bible. Others have decided to study the Bible when shown what it says about the purpose of life, why God permits wickedness, the significance of current events, or the hope of eternal life on a paradise earth. In lands where religious practices have exposed people to harassment by evil spirits, the Bible's explanation of what causes this and how to gain relief has aroused interest. Why do these points impress sincere people? Because the Bible is the only source of reliable information on all such vital matters.—Psalm 119:130.

5 However, what if people tell us that they do not be-

---

3. What is the best way to help many who are not convinced that the Bible is the Word of God?
4. What explanations of Bible truths have changed the attitude of some people toward the Bible, and why?
5. (a) When people say that they do not believe the Bible, what may be the reasons? (b) How might we help such people?

lieve the Bible? Should that end the conversation? Not if they are willing to reason. It may be that they view the Bible as Christendom's book. Her record of hypocrisy and political meddling, as well as her constant solicitations for money, may account for their negative reaction to the Bible. Why not ask if that is so? The Bible's condemnation of Christendom's worldly ways, along with points of contrast between Christendom and true Christianity, may arouse their interest.—Micah 3:11, 12; Matthew 15:7-9; James 4:4.

6 For others, a straightforward discussion of the evidences that the Bible is inspired of God may be helpful. What clearly proves to *you* that the Bible is from Jehovah God? Is it what the Bible itself says as to its origin? Or is it the fact that the Bible contains numerous prophecies reflecting detailed knowledge of the future, prophecies that must have come from a superhuman source? (2 Peter 1:20, 21) Is it perhaps that the Bible displays wonderful internal harmony, although written down by 40 men over a period of some 1,600 years? Or its scientific accuracy in contrast with other writings from those times? Or the candor of its writers? Or its preservation in the face of vicious efforts to destroy it? Whatever you have personally found to be impressive can also be used to help other people.*

---

* For a discussion of why the Bible merits consideration, see the brochure *A Book for All People,* published by Jehovah's Witnesses.

---

6. (a) What convinces you personally that the Bible is God's Word? (b) What other lines of reasoning can be used to help people appreciate that the Bible really is from God?

Our Bible Reading

7 In addition to helping others believe the Bible, we ourselves need to take time to read it regularly. Are you doing that? Of all the books ever produced, this one is the most important. Of course, this does not mean that if we read it on our own, we need nothing else. The Scriptures warn against isolating ourselves. We should not think that we can figure out everything by independent research. Both personal study and regular attendance at the meetings of God's people are needed if we are to be balanced Christians.—Proverbs 18:1; Hebrews 10:24, 25.

8 Regarding this, the Bible tells about an Ethiopian official who was reading from the prophecy of Isaiah. An angel directed the Christian evangelizer Philip to ask the man: "Do you actually know what you are reading?" Humbly, the Ethiopian replied: "Really, how could I ever do so, unless someone guided me?" He urged Philip to explain the passage of Scripture. Now, Philip was not merely an independent Bible reader who gave his opinion on the Scriptures. He maintained close contact with God's visible organization. So he could help the Ethiopian to benefit from the instruction that Jehovah was making available through that organization. (Acts 6:5, 6; 8:5, 26-35) Similarly today, no one arrives at a correct understanding of Jehovah's purposes on his own. We all need the aid that

---

7, 8. (a) What should we be doing with the Bible? (b) What do we need in addition to personal Bible reading? (c) How have you personally gained an understanding of Jehovah's purposes?

Jehovah lovingly provides through his visible organization.

9 To help us understand the Bible, Jehovah's organization supplies excellent Scriptural material in various publications. In addition, a regular schedule of Bible reading is set out for us in connection with the Theocratic Ministry School held in all the congregations of Jehovah's Witnesses throughout the world. Great benefit can come from personally examining the Holy Scriptures. (Psalm 1:1-3; 19:7, 8) Make a special effort to read the Bible regularly. Even though you do not fully understand everything, your getting an overall view of the Scriptures will be of great value. For example, if you read only four or five pages a day, you can complete the Bible in about a year.

10 When can you do your Bible reading? If you set aside even 10 or 15 minutes a day for it, you will be greatly benefited. If not, at least schedule regular times for it each week, and then hold to that schedule. If you are married, you and your mate can enjoy reading the Bible aloud to each other. If there are children old enough to read, they may take turns reading aloud. Bible reading should be a lifelong habit, like eating food. As you know, if a person's eating habits are poor, his health will suffer. So, too, our spiritual life, and hence our eternal life, depends on our being regularly nourished on "every utterance coming forth through Jehovah's mouth."—Matthew 4:4.

---

9. What program of Bible reading can benefit all of us?
10. (a) When do you do your Bible reading? (b) Who else should be included when reading the Bible, and why is regularity important?

Our Objective

11 What should be our objective in reading the Bible? Our goal should not be simply to cover a certain number of pages. Our motive should be to know God better so that we can increase our love for him and worship him acceptably. (John 5:39-42) Our attitude should be like that of the Bible writer who said: "Make me know your own ways, O Jehovah; teach me your own paths."—Psalm 25:4.

12 As we receive teachings from Jehovah, it should be our desire to gain "accurate knowledge." Without it, how could we apply God's Word properly in our own lives or explain it correctly to others? (Colossians 3:10; 2 Timothy 2:15) Gaining *accurate* knowledge requires that we read carefully, and if a portion is deep, we may need to read it more than once in order to grasp the sense of it. We will also be benefited if we take time to meditate on the material, thinking about it from various standpoints. Four valuable avenues of thought to explore are highlighted on page 30. Many portions of Scripture can beneficially be analyzed by using one or more of these viewpoints. As you answer the questions on the following pages, you will see how that is so.

(1) ***Often, the portion of Scripture that you are reading can tell you something about the kind of person Jehovah is.***

---

11. What should be our objective in reading the Bible?
12. (a) Why is gaining "accurate knowledge" necessary, and what effort when reading may be needed in order to get that knowledge? (b) By using what four viewpoints might we beneficially analyze what we read in the Bible? (See box on page 30.) (c) Illustrate these points by answering the questions provided in this paragraph. Look up the scriptures cited but not quoted.

For example, at Psalm 139:13, 14, we learn of God's great concern for the unborn: "You kept me screened off in the belly of my mother. I shall laud you because in a fear-inspiring way I am wonderfully made. Your works are wonderful, as my soul is very well aware." How marvelous Jehovah's creative works are! The way humans are made testifies to his great love for us.

In view of what is said at John 14:9, 10, when we read how Jesus dealt with others, we are really seeing how Jehovah himself would act. With that in mind, what can we conclude about Jehovah from the incidents recorded at Luke 5:12, 13 and Luke 7: 11-15?

(2) *Consider how the account contributes to the Bible's theme: the vindication of Jehovah's sovereignty and the sanctification of his name by the Kingdom under Jesus Christ, the promised Seed.*

How was the Bible's theme emphasized by Ezekiel and Daniel? (Ezekiel 38:21-23; Daniel 2:44; 4:17; 7: 9-14)

How does the Bible clearly identify Jesus as the promised Seed? (Galatians 3:16)

How does Revelation describe the grand climax of the Kingdom theme? (Revelation 11:15; 12:7-10; 17:16-18; 19:11-16; 20:1-3; 21:1-5)

(3) *Ask yourself how you can make personal application of what you are reading.* For example, we read in Exodus through Deuteronomy about Israel's immorality and rebelliousness. We learn that those attitudes and actions brought bad consequences. Thus, we should be

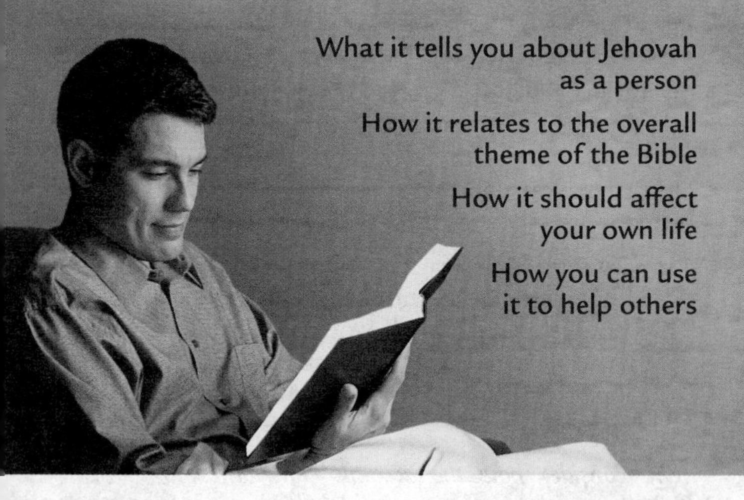

moved to please Jehovah by not imitating Israel's bad example. "These things went on befalling them as examples, and they were written for a warning to us upon whom the ends of the systems of things have arrived."—1 Corinthians 10:11.

The record about Cain's killing Abel has what lesson for us? (Genesis 4:3-12; Hebrews 11:4; 1 John 3: 10-15; 4:20, 21)

Does Bible counsel to Christians who have a heavenly hope apply also to those who have the hope of eternal life on earth? (Numbers 15:16; John 10:16)

Even though we are in good standing in the Christian congregation, why do we need to consider how to apply more fully the Bible counsel that we already know? (2 Corinthians 13:5; 1 Thessalonians 4:1)

(4) ***Give thought to how you might use what you are reading to help others.*** All people are concerned about health problems, so we can read with them what Jesus did to illustrate what he will do on a much larger scale in Kingdom power: "Great crowds approached him, having along with them people that were lame, maimed, blind, dumb, and many otherwise, . . . and he cured them."—Matthew 15:30.

Who might be helped by the account of the resurrection of the daughter of Jairus? (Luke 8:41, 42, 49-56)

13 How richly rewarding Bible reading becomes when we consider the four points mentioned above! To be sure, reading the Bible is a challenge. But it can benefit us for a lifetime, for as we read the Scriptures, we will grow stronger spiritually. Regular Bible reading will draw us closer to our loving Father, Jehovah, and to our Christian brothers. It will help us in heeding the counsel to keep "a tight grip on the word of life."—Philippians 2:16.

---

13. What results can we expect from a continuing program of Bible reading and study with Jehovah's organization?

Review Discussion

- Why was the Bible written and preserved until our day?
- How can we help others to appreciate the Bible?
- Why is regular personal Bible reading profitable? By using what four viewpoints might we beneficially analyze what we read?

CHAPTER FOUR

The One to Whom All the Prophets Bore Witness

"THE Father has affection for the Son and shows him all the things he himself does." (John 5:20) What a warm relationship the Son enjoyed with his Father, Jehovah! The closeness of that relationship began at the time of his creation, countless millenniums before his human birth. He was God's only-begotten Son, the only one created directly by Jehovah himself. Everything else in heaven and on earth was created by means of that dearly loved firstborn Son. (Colossians 1:15, 16) He also served as God's Word, or Spokesman, the One through whom the divine will was communicated to others. This one, the Son that God was specially fond of, became the man Jesus Christ.—Proverbs 8:22-30; John 1:14, 18; 12:49, 50.

2 Before God's firstborn Son was miraculously conceived as a human, scores of inspired prophecies were recorded about him. The apostle Peter testified to Cornelius: "To him all the prophets bear witness." (Acts 10:43) The role of Jesus was featured in the Bible to such an extent that an angel told the apostle John: "The bearing witness to Jesus is what inspires prophesying." (Revelation 19:10) Those prophecies clearly

---

1. What do the facts about Jesus' prehuman existence show as to his relationship with Jehovah?
2. To what extent have Bible prophecies referred to Jesus?

identified him as the Messiah. They drew attention to various roles he would play in fulfilling God's purposes. All of this should be of keen interest to us today.

What the Prophecies Revealed

3 The first of such prophecies was spoken after the rebellion in Eden. Jehovah said to the serpent: "I shall put enmity between you and the woman and between your seed and her seed. He will bruise you in the head and you will bruise him in the heel." (Genesis 3:15) That prophecy was really addressed to Satan, the one represented by the serpent. "The woman" is Jehovah's own loyal heavenly organization, which is like a faithful wife to him. The 'seed of the serpent' includes all angels and humans who manifest the spirit of Satan, those who oppose Jehovah and His people. The 'bruising of the serpent in the head' means the eventual destruction of the rebel Satan, who slandered Jehovah and brought great grief to mankind. But what is the identity of the principal part of the "seed" who would do the bruising? For centuries, that remained a "sacred secret."—Romans 16:20, 25, 26.

4 After some 2,000 years of human history, Jehovah provided further details. He indicated that the Seed would appear in the family line of Abraham. (Genesis 22:15-18) However, the line leading to the Seed would depend, not on fleshly descent, but on God's choice.

---

3. (a) In the prophecy at Genesis 3:15, who is represented by the serpent, "the woman," and the 'seed of the serpent'? (b) Why would the 'bruising of the serpent in the head' be of great interest to Jehovah's servants?
4. How did Jesus' ancestry help to identify him as the promised Seed?

In spite of Abraham's love for his son Ishmael, born to Hagar, Jehovah said: "My covenant I shall establish with Isaac, whom Sarah will bear to you." (Genesis 17:18-21) Later that covenant was confirmed, not to Isaac's firstborn son, Esau, but to Jacob, from whom the 12 tribes of Israel descended. (Genesis 28:10-14) In time, it was indicated that the Seed would be born in the tribe of Judah, in the line of David.—Genesis 49:10; 1 Chronicles 17:3, 4, 11-14.

5 What other clues were given as to the Seed's identity? Over 700 years in advance, the Bible named Bethlehem as the place of the human birth of the promised Seed. It also revealed that the Seed had already existed "from the days of time indefinite," since the time he was created in heaven. (Micah 5:2) The exact time of his appearance on earth as the Messiah was also foretold, through the prophet Daniel. (Daniel 9:24-26) And when Jesus was anointed with holy spirit, actually becoming Jehovah's Anointed One, God's own voice from heaven clearly identified him as His Son. (Matthew 3:16, 17) The Seed was revealed! Thus, Philip could say with conviction: "We have found the one of whom Moses, in the Law, and the Prophets wrote, Jesus."—John 1:45.

6 Thereafter, Jesus' followers came to realize that literally scores of prophetic references to him had been woven into the inspired Scriptures. (Luke 24:27) It be-

---

5. When Jesus began his earthly ministry, what made it evident that he was the Messiah?

6. (a) According to Luke 24:27, what did Jesus' followers come to realize? (b) Who is the principal part of the 'seed of the woman,' and what is meant by his bruising the serpent's head?

came even clearer that Jesus is the principal part of the 'seed of the woman,' the one who will bruise the head of the serpent, crushing Satan out of existence. By means of Jesus, all of God's promises to humankind, all the things for which we earnestly long, will be brought to fulfillment.—2 Corinthians 1:20.

7 How should knowing this affect us? The Bible tells of an Ethiopian eunuch who had read some of these prophecies about the coming Redeemer and Messiah. Puzzled, he asked the evangelizer Philip: "About whom does the prophet say this?" But the eunuch did not let the matter rest when he received the answer. After listening carefully to the explanation that Philip gave, the man realized that appreciation for this fulfilled prophecy called for action on his own part. He understood that he needed to get baptized. (Acts 8:32-38; Isaiah 53:3-9) Do we respond similarly?

8 Consider, too, the touching account of Abraham's attempt to offer up Isaac, his only son by Sarah. (Genesis 22:1-18) That foreshadowed what Jehovah would do—offer up his only-begotten Son: "God loved the world so much that he gave his only-begotten Son, in order that everyone exercising faith in him might not be destroyed but have everlasting life." (John 3:16) This gives us confidence that just as Jehovah gave his only-begotten Son to fulfill His purpose, He will also

---

7. In addition to the identity of the One referred to in the prophecies, what else is it beneficial to realize?
8. (a) What did Abraham's attempt to offer up Isaac foreshadow? (b) Why did Jehovah tell Abraham that all nations would bless themselves by means of the Seed, and how does this apply to us today?

"kindly give us all other things." (Romans 8:32) What is required on our part? As recorded at Genesis 22: 18, Jehovah told Abraham that all nations would bless themselves by means of the Seed, "due to the fact that [Abraham had] listened to [God's] voice." We too need to listen to Jehovah and to his Son: "He that exercises faith in the Son has everlasting life; he that disobeys the Son will not see life, but the wrath of God remains upon him."—John 3:36.

Jesus told his followers that they should teach others to observe God's commandments

9 If we appreciate the hope of everlasting life made possible by Jesus' sacrifice, we will want to do the things that Jehovah has spoken to us through Jesus. These revolve around our love for God and for our neighbors. (Matthew 22:37-39) Jesus showed that our love for Jehovah would motivate us to teach others "to observe all the things [that Jesus has] commanded [us]." (Matthew 28:19, 20) And we want to share that love with fellow servants of Jehovah by the regular "gathering of ourselves together" with them. (Hebrews 10:25; Galatians 6:10) Too, in listening to God and his Son, we should not think that they demand perfection from us. Hebrews 4:15 says that Jesus, as our High Priest, can "sympathize with our weaknesses." How comforting that is, especially when we approach God in prayer through Christ for help to overcome our weaknesses!—Matthew 6:12.

Show Faith in Christ

10 After pointing out to the Jewish high court in Jerusalem that Bible prophecy had been fulfilled in Jesus, the apostle Peter forcefully concluded: "There is no salvation in anyone else, for there is not another name under heaven that has been given among men by which we must get saved." (Acts 4:12) Since all of Adam's offspring are sinners, their death holds no merit that can be applied as a ransom for anyone. But Jesus was perfect, and his life had sacrificial value. (Psalm 49:6-9; Hebrews 2:9) He offered to

---

9. If we appreciate the hope of everlasting life made possible by Jesus' sacrifice, what will we do?
10. Why is there no salvation apart from Jesus Christ?

God a ransom that exactly corresponded in value to the perfect life that Adam had lost. (1 Timothy 2:5, 6) This opened the way for us to obtain everlasting life in God's new world.

11 The ransom also opened the way for us to receive other benefits, even now. For example, although we are sinners, Jesus' sacrifice makes possible our having a clean conscience because of forgiveness of sin. This is far more than was ever achieved for the Israelites by the animal sacrifices that the Mosaic Law required. (Acts 13:38, 39; Hebrews 9:13, 14; 10:22) However, having such forgiveness requires that we honestly recognize how much we need Christ's sacrifice: "If we make the statement: 'We have no sin,' we are misleading ourselves and the truth is not in us. If we confess our sins, he is faithful and righteous so as to forgive us our sins and to cleanse us from all unrighteousness." —1 John 1:8, 9.

12 How can sinners express faith in Christ and his sacrifice? When people in the first century became believers, they publicly demonstrated that. How? They got baptized. Why? Because Jesus commanded that all his disciples be baptized. (Matthew 28:19, 20; Acts 8: 12; 18:8) A person will not hold back when his heart is really moved by the loving provision that Jehovah made through Jesus. He will make any needed adjustments in his life, dedicate himself to God in prayer, and symbolize his dedication by water immersion. It is

---

11. Explain how Jesus' sacrifice can greatly benefit us.
12. Why is water immersion an important factor in gaining a good conscience before God?

by demonstrating faith in this way that he makes 're-quest to God for a good conscience.'—1 Peter 3:21.

13 Even after this, of course, sinful traits will show themselves. What then? The apostle John said: "I am writing you these things that you may not commit a sin. And yet, if anyone does commit a sin, we have a helper with the Father, Jesus Christ, a righteous one. And he is a propitiatory sacrifice for our sins." (1 John 2:1, 2) Does this mean that no matter what we do, if we pray to God for forgiveness, everything will be all right? Not necessarily. The key to forgiveness is genuine repentance. Help may also be needed from older, more experienced ones in the Christian congregation. We must recognize the wrongness of what was done and feel sincere regret over it so that we will make an earnest effort to avoid repeating it. (Acts 3:19; James 5: 13-16) If we do this, we can be assured of Jesus' help and of our restoration to Jehovah's favor.

14 Jesus' sacrifice has opened the way for eternal life in heaven for a "little flock," the subsidiary part of the seed of Genesis 3:15. (Luke 12:32; Galatians 3:26-29) It has also opened the way for eternal life on a paradise earth for billions of others of mankind. (Psalm 37: 29; Revelation 20:11, 12; 21:3, 4) Eternal life is "the gift God gives . . . by Christ Jesus our Lord." (Romans 6: 23; Ephesians 2:8-10) If we have faith in that gift and appreciation for the manner in which it was made possible, we will make this manifest. Discerning how

---

13. If we realize that we have committed a sin, what should we do about it, and why?

14. (a) Explain an important way in which Jesus' sacrifice has benefited us. (b) If we really have faith, what will we do?

marvelously Jehovah has used Jesus in accomplishing His will and how vital it is that all of us follow Jesus' steps closely, we will make the Christian ministry one of the most important activities in our life. Our faith will be evident from the conviction with which we tell others about this magnificent gift from God. —Acts 20:24.

15 What a fine, unifying effect such faith has! By means of it, we are drawn closer to Jehovah, to his Son, and to one another within the Christian congregation. (1 John 3:23, 24) It causes us to rejoice that Jehovah has kindly given to his Son "the name that is above every other name [except God's name], so that in the name of Jesus every knee should bend of those in heaven and those on earth and those under the ground, and every tongue should openly acknowledge that Jesus Christ is Lord to the glory of God the Father."—Philippians 2:9-11.

---

15. How does faith in Jesus Christ have a unifying effect?

Review Discussion

- When the Messiah appeared, why was his identity clear to those who truly believed God's Word?
- What are some of the things we should do to show our appreciation for Jesus' sacrifice?
- In what ways has Jesus' sacrifice already benefited us? How does this help us when we pray to Jehovah for forgiveness of sins?

CHAPTER FIVE

Freedom Enjoyed by Worshipers of Jehovah

WHEN Jehovah created the first man and woman, they enjoyed freedom far surpassing any that humans have today. Their home was Paradise, the beautiful Garden of Eden. No illness marred their enjoyment of life, as they had perfect minds and bodies. Death was not waiting for them as it has for everyone since then. Also, they were not robots but had the marvelous gift of free will, the ability to make their own decisions. To continue to enjoy such wonderful freedom, however, they had to respect God's laws.

2 Consider, for example, the physical laws God has put in place. Of course, these laws may not have been stated in so many words, but Adam and Eve were made in such a way that it was only natural to obey them. Their appetite signaled the need to eat; their thirst, the need to drink; the setting of the sun, the need to sleep. Jehovah also gave them an assignment of work. That assignment was, in effect, a law because it would govern their course of action. They were to bring forth children, exercise dominion over earth's many forms of life, and extend the borders of Paradise until it covered the entire globe. (Genesis 1:28; 2:15) What a kindly, beneficial law

---

1, 2. (a) What kind of freedom did God give the first human pair? (b) Mention some of the laws that governed the activity of Adam and Eve.

that was! It gave them thoroughly satisfying work, enabling them to use their faculties to the full in wholesome ways. Also, they had ample leeway to make decisions as to how they would carry out their assignment. What more could anyone ask?

3 Of course, when Adam and Eve were granted the privilege of making decisions, this did not mean that just any decision they might make would produce good results. Their freedom to make decisions was to be exercised within the boundaries of God's laws and principles. How could they learn these? By listening to their Maker and by observing his works. God gave Adam and Eve the intelligence needed to apply what they learned. Since they were created perfect, their natural inclination would be to reflect God's qualities when making decisions. Indeed, they would be careful to do that if they truly appreciated what God had done for them and wanted to please him.—Genesis 1:26, 27; John 8:29.

4 Rightly, then, God chose to test their devotion to him as their Life-Giver and their willingness to remain within the area decreed by him. Jehovah gave Adam this command: "From every tree of the garden you may eat to satisfaction. But as for the tree of the knowledge of good and bad you must not eat from it, for in the day you eat from it you will positively die." (Genesis 2:16, 17) After Eve's creation, she too was informed of this law. (Genesis 3:2, 3) Did this restriction deprive them of

---

3. How could Adam and Eve learn to use wisely their freedom to make decisions?

4. (a) Did the command given to Adam and Eve not to eat of the fruit of one tree deprive them of freedom? (b) Why was this a fitting requirement?

freedom? Certainly not. They had an abundance of delightful food of all kinds to eat without eating the fruit of that one tree. (Genesis 2:8, 9) It was only fitting that they should recognize that the earth belongs to God, since he created it. So he has the right to make laws that suit his purpose and that benefit mankind.—Psalm 24: 1, 10.

5 But what happened? Motivated by selfish ambition, an angel misused his free will and became Satan, which means "Resister." He deceived Eve by assuring her of something contrary to God's will. (Genesis 3:4, 5) Adam joined Eve in breaking God's law. By grasping for what did not belong to them, they lost their glorious freedom. Sin became their master, and as God had warned, death eventually followed. The inheritance they passed on to their offspring was sin—manifest in an inborn tendency toward wrongdoing. Sin also brought weaknesses resulting in disease, aging, and death. The inclination toward wrongdoing, aggravated by Satanic influence, produced a human society with a history of hatreds, crimes, oppression, and wars that have taken many millions of lives. What a contrast to the freedom that God gave mankind at the beginning!—Deuteronomy 32:4, 5; Job 14:1, 2; Romans 5:12; Revelation 12:9.

Where Freedom Can Be Found

6 In view of the bad conditions that exist everywhere today, it is no surprise that people long for greater

---

5. (a) How did Adam and Eve lose the glorious freedom they had? (b) What took the place of the freedom Adam and Eve had enjoyed, and how have we been affected?
6. (a) Where can real freedom be found? (b) What kind of freedom did Jesus speak about?

freedom. But where can real freedom be found? Jesus said: "If you remain in my word, you are really my disciples, and you will know the truth, and the truth will set you free." (John 8:31, 32) This freedom is not the kind that men hope for when they reject one ruler or one form of government in favor of another. Instead, this freedom gets right to the core of human problems. What Jesus was discussing was freedom from bondage to sin. (John 8:24, 34-36) Thus, if a person becomes a true disciple of Jesus Christ, he experiences a notable change in his life, a liberation!

7 This does not mean that at present true Christians no longer feel the effects of the inborn tendency toward sinful conduct. Since they have inherited sin, they still have a struggle because of it. (Romans 7:21-25) If a person really lives in harmony with Jesus' teachings, however, he will no longer be a slave to sin. No longer will sin be to him like a dictator who gives him orders that he must blindly obey. He will not be trapped in a way of life that lacks purpose and that leaves him with a bad conscience. He will enjoy a clean conscience before God because past sins have been forgiven on the basis of his faith in the sacrifice of Christ. Sinful inclinations may try to assert themselves, but when he refuses to act on them because he calls to mind the clean teachings of Christ, he shows that sin is no longer his master.—Romans 6:12-17.

8 Consider the freedoms we enjoy as Christians. We

---

7. (a) In what sense can we be free from sin now? (b) To have that freedom, what must we do?
8. (a) What freedoms does true Christianity give us? (b) What should our attitude be toward secular rulers?

have been liberated from the effects of false teachings, from bondage to superstition, and from servitude to sin. The grand truths about the condition of the dead and the resurrection have freed us from unreasoning fear of death. Knowledge that imperfect human governments will soon be replaced by God's righteous Kingdom frees us from hopelessness. (Daniel 2:44; Matthew 6:10) However, such freedom does not justify disrespect for governmental authorities and their laws.—Titus 3:1, 2; 1 Peter 2:16, 17.

9 Jehovah does not make us figure out by trial and error what is the best way to live. He knows how we are made, what brings us genuine contentment, and what is to our eternal benefit. He is aware of thoughts and conduct that can spoil a person's relationship with Him and with fellow humans, perhaps even barring that person from the new world. Lovingly, Jehovah informs us of all these things by means of the Bible and his visible organization. (Mark 13:10; Galatians 5:19-23; 1 Timothy 1:12, 13) Then it is up to us to use our God-given free will to decide how we are going to respond. Unlike Adam, if we have taken to heart what the Bible tells us, we will make wise decisions. We will show that a good relationship with Jehovah is our main concern in life.

Wanting Another Kind of Freedom

10 At times some young people who are Jehovah's

---

9. (a) How does Jehovah lovingly help us to enjoy the greatest measure of freedom now possible for humans? (b) How can we make wise decisions?
10. What kind of freedom have some who are Jehovah's Witnesses reached out for?

Witnesses—as well as others not so young—may feel that they want another kind of freedom. The world may appear to be glamorous, and the more they think about it, the stronger becomes their desire to do the unchristian things that are popular in the world. Such ones may not plan to abuse drugs, drink too much, or commit fornication. But they begin to associate with some who are not true Christians, wanting to be accepted by these. They may even begin to imitate their speech and conduct.—3 John 11.

11 Sometimes the enticement to indulge in unchristian conduct comes from someone who professes to serve Jehovah. That was true of some early Christians, and the same thing can happen in our day. Such people

---

11. From where does the enticement to do wrong sometimes come?

often want to do things that they feel will bring them pleasure, but these things are against God's laws. They urge others to have some "fun." They 'promise freedom, while they themselves are slaves of corruption.' —2 Peter 2:19.

12 The fruitage of such so-called freedom is always bad, since it means disobeying God's laws. For example, illicit sex can result in emotional turmoil, disease, death, unwanted pregnancy, and possibly the breakup of a marriage. (1 Corinthians 6:18; 1 Thessalonians 4:3-8) Drug abuse can produce irritability, slurred speech, blurred vision, dizziness, impaired ability to breathe, hallucinations, and death. It can result in addiction, which may lead to crime in order to support the habit. Much the same consequences come from alcohol abuse. (Proverbs 23:29-35) Those who get involved in such conduct may think that they are free, but then they find out too late that they have become slaves to sin. And what a cruel master sin is! Reasoning on the matter *now* can help to safeguard us against such an experience.—Galatians 6:7, 8.

Where Problems Begin

13 Think about where problems often begin. The Bible explains: "Each one is tried by being drawn out and enticed by his own desire. Then the desire, when it has

---

12. What are the sad results of conduct contrary to God's laws and principles?

13. (a) How do the desires that lead to problems often get stirred up? (b) To understand what "bad associations" are, whose viewpoint do we need? (c) As you answer the questions listed in paragraph 13, emphasize Jehovah's viewpoint.

become fertile, gives birth to sin; in turn, sin, when it has been accomplished, brings forth death." (James 1:14, 15) How does the desire get stirred up? By what goes into the mind. Often this is a result of associating with people who do not apply Bible principles. Of course, we all know that we should avoid "bad associations." (1 Corinthians 15:33) But which associations are bad? How does Jehovah view the matter? Reasoning on the following questions and looking up the scriptures cited should help us to arrive at proper conclusions.

Does the fact that certain people seem to be honorable mean that they are good associates? (Genesis 34:1, 2, 18, 19)

Could their conversation, perhaps their jokes, indicate whether we belong in close company with them? (Ephesians 5:3, 4)

How does Jehovah feel if we choose intimate association with people who do not love him? (2 Chronicles 19:1, 2)

Although we may work with or go to school with people who do not share our beliefs, why is there a need for us to be cautious? (1 Peter 4:3, 4)

Viewing television and movies, using the Internet, and reading books, magazines, and newspapers are ways of associating with others. Against what type of material from such sources need we be on guard? (Proverbs 3:31; Isaiah 8:19; Ephesians 4:17-19)

What does our choice of associates tell Jehovah as to the kind of people we are? (Psalm 26:1, 4, 5; 97:10)

14 Immediately ahead of us lies God's new world. By means of God's heavenly Kingdom government, mankind will be freed from the influence of Satan and his entire wicked system of things. Gradually, all the effects of sin will be removed from obedient mankind, resulting in perfection of mind and body, so that we will be able to enjoy everlasting life in Paradise. Freedom that is in full harmony with "the spirit of Jehovah" will eventually be enjoyed by all creation. (2 Corinthians 3:17) Would it make sense to risk losing all of that because of disregarding the counsel of God's Word now? By exercising our Christian freedom wisely today, may we all show clearly that what we really want is "the glorious freedom of the children of God."—Romans 8:21.

---

14. What grand freedom lies ahead for those who faithfully apply the counsel of God's Word now?

Review Discussion

- What kind of freedom did the first human pair enjoy? How does that compare with what mankind is experiencing now?
- What freedom do true Christians have? How does this contrast with what the world considers freedom?
- Why is it so important to avoid bad associations? Unlike Adam, whose decisions as to what is bad do we accept?

CHAPTER SIX

The Issue That We All Have to Face

YOU are involved in the most important issue ever to face mankind. Where you stand on it will determine your everlasting future. This issue was raised when rebellion broke out in Eden. Back then Satan asked Eve: "Is it really so that God said you must not eat from every tree of the garden?" She replied that concerning one tree God had said: "You must not eat from it . . . that you do not die." Then Satan directly charged Jehovah with lying, saying that neither Eve's life nor Adam's life was dependent on obedience to God. Satan claimed that God was withholding from his creatures something good—the ability to set their own standards in life. Satan asserted: "God knows that in the very day of your eating from it your eyes are bound to be opened and you are bound to be like God, knowing good and bad."—Genesis 3:1-5.

2 In effect, Satan was saying that humans would be better off making their own decisions rather than obeying God's laws. He thus challenged God's way of ruling. This raised the all-important issue of God's universal sovereignty, that is, his right to rule. The question was raised: Which is better for humans, Jeho-

---

1, 2. (a) What issue did Satan raise in Eden? (b) How is that issue implied by what he said?

vah's way of ruling or rulership independent of him? Now, Jehovah could have immediately executed Adam and Eve, but that would hardly have settled the issue of sovereignty satisfactorily. By letting human society develop for a considerable time, God could demonstrate just what independence from him and his laws would produce.

3 Satan's attack on Jehovah's right to rule did not stop with what took place in Eden. He called into question loyalty to Jehovah on the part of others. This became a closely related secondary issue. His challenge reached out to include both the offspring of Adam and Eve and all the spirit sons of God, even Jehovah's dearly loved firstborn Son. In the days of Job, for instance, Satan contended that those who serve Jehovah do so, not out of love for God and his way of ruling, but for selfish reasons. He argued that when subjected to hardship, they would all give in to selfish desires. —Job 2:1-6; Revelation 12:10.

What History Has Proved

4 A vital point in the issue of sovereignty is this: God did not create humans to live independently of his rulership and be successful. For their benefit he made them dependent on his righteous laws. The prophet Jeremiah acknowledged: "I well know, O Jehovah, that to earthling man his way does not belong. It does not belong to man who is walking even to direct his step. Correct me, O Jehovah." (Jeremiah 10:23, 24) So God's

---

3. What secondary issue did Satan raise?

4, 5. What has history proved about man directing his own steps?

Word urges: "Trust in Jehovah with all your heart and do not lean upon your own understanding." (Proverbs 3:5) Just as God made humankind subject to his physical laws to stay alive, he also made moral laws, which if obeyed would make for a harmonious society.

5 Clearly, God knew that the human family could never be successful in regulating itself without his rulership. In a vain attempt to be independent of God's rule, humans have set up different political, economic, and religious systems. These differences have brought people into constant conflict with one another, resulting in violence, war, and death. "Man has dominated man to his injury." (Ecclesiastes 8:9) That is just what has happened throughout human history. As foretold in God's Word, wicked men and impostors have continued to "advance from bad to worse." (2 Timothy 3: 13) And the 20th century, which saw mankind reach great heights in scientific and industrial achievement, saw the worst calamities ever. The words of Jeremiah 10:23 have been abundantly proved—humans were not created to direct their own steps.

6 The tragic, long-term consequences of independence from God have once and for all demonstrated that rulership by humans can never succeed. God's rulership is the only way to happiness, unity, health, and life. And God's Word shows that Jehovah's toleration of independent human rule is nearing its end. (Matthew 24:3-14; 2 Timothy 3:1-5) Shortly, he will intervene in human affairs to assert his rulership over the earth. Bible prophecy states: "In the days of those

---

6. How will God soon resolve human independence from him?

kings [human rulerships now existing] the God of heaven will set up a kingdom [in heaven] that will never be brought to ruin. And the kingdom itself will not be passed on to any other people [never again will humans rule the earth]. It will crush and put an end to all these [present-day] kingdoms, and it itself will stand to times indefinite."—Daniel 2:44.

Surviving Into God's New World

7 When God's rule ends man's rule, who will survive? The Bible answers: "The upright [those who uphold God's right to rule] are the ones that will reside in the earth, and the blameless are the ones that will be left over in it. As regards the wicked [those who do not uphold God's right to rule], they will be cut off from the very earth." (Proverbs 2:21, 22) Similarly, the psalmist stated: "Just a little while longer, and the wicked one will be no more . . . The righteous themselves will possess the earth, and they will reside forever upon it." —Psalm 37:10, 29.

8 After Satan's system is destroyed, God will usher in his new world, which will completely eliminate the devastating violence, wars, poverty, suffering, sickness, and death that have held mankind in their grip for thousands of years. The Bible beautifully describes the blessings awaiting obedient mankind: "He [God] will wipe out every tear from their eyes, and death will be no more, neither will mourning nor outcry nor pain be anymore. The former things have passed away." (Revelation 21:3, 4) By means of his heavenly Kingdom

---

7. When God's rule ends man's rule, who will survive?
8. How will God fully vindicate his sovereignty?

government under Christ, God will fully vindicate (justify, or prove) His right to be our Sovereign, that is, our Ruler.—Romans 16:20; 2 Peter 3:10-13; Revelation 20:1-6.

How They Responded to the Issue

9 Down through history, there have been men and women of faith who have proved their loyalty to Jehovah as Sovereign. They knew that their lives depended on listening to and obeying him. Noah was such a man. So God said to Noah: "The end of all flesh has come before me . . . Make for yourself an ark." And Noah submitted to Jehovah's direction. Despite being given warning, other people of that day went about their lives as if nothing unusual was going to happen. But Noah built a gigantic ark and kept busy preaching to others about Jehovah's righteous ways. The record goes on to say: "Noah proceeded to do according to all that God had commanded him. He did just so."—Genesis 6:13-22; Hebrews 11:7; 2 Peter 2:5.

10 Abraham and Sarah were also fine examples of upholding Jehovah's sovereignty, doing whatever he commanded them. They lived in Ur of the Chaldeans, a prosperous city. But when Jehovah told Abraham to go to another land, one that he was not familiar with, Abraham "went just as Jehovah had spoken to him."

---

9. (a) How have those who have remained loyal to Jehovah viewed his word? (b) How did Noah prove his loyalty, and how can we benefit from his example?

10. (a) How did Abraham and Sarah uphold Jehovah's sovereignty? (b) In what way can we benefit from the examples of Abraham and Sarah?

Sarah no doubt had had a comfortable way of life —with home, friends, and relatives. Yet, she was submissive to Jehovah and to her husband and went to the land of Canaan, although she did not know what conditions awaited her there.—Genesis 11:31–12:4; Acts 7: 2-4.

11 Moses was another person who upheld Jehovah's sovereignty. And he did this under the most difficult circumstances—in face-to-face confrontations with Pharaoh of Egypt. Not that Moses was self-confident. On the contrary, he doubted his ability to speak well enough. But he obeyed Jehovah. With Jehovah's backing and the aid of his brother, Aaron, Moses repeatedly delivered Jehovah's word to obstinate Pharaoh. Even some of the sons of Israel were harshly critical of Moses. Yet, Moses loyally did everything that Jehovah commanded him, and by means of him, Israel was delivered from Egypt.—Exodus 7:6; 12:50, 51; Hebrews 11:24-27.

12 Those who were loyal to Jehovah did not reason that all that was required was to obey what God had put in writing. When Potiphar's wife tried to entice Joseph to have adulterous relations with her, there was no written commandment from God that prohibited adultery. However, Joseph knew about the marriage arrangement instituted by Jehovah in Eden. He was

---

11. (a) Under what circumstances did Moses uphold Jehovah's sovereignty? (b) How might Moses' example benefit us?

12. (a) What shows that loyalty to Jehovah involves more than doing what God has specified in writing? (b) How might appreciation of this kind of loyalty help us to apply 1 John 2:15?

aware that having sexual relations with another man's wife would be displeasing to God. Joseph was not interested in testing the limits to which God would let him be like the Egyptians. He upheld Jehovah's ways by meditating on God's dealings with mankind and then conscientiously applying what he discerned to be God's will.—Genesis 39:7-12; Psalm 77:11, 12.

13 Even if severely put to the test, those who truly know Jehovah do not turn away from him. Satan charged that if Job lost his many possessions or his health, even he—of whom Jehovah spoke highly—would desert God. But Job proved the Devil a liar, even though Job himself did not know why calamities were engulfing him. (Job 2:9, 10) Centuries later, still trying to prove his point, Satan caused an infuriated king of Babylon to threaten three young Hebrews with death in a fiery furnace if they did not bow in worship before an image set up by the king. Forced to choose between obedience to the command of the king and obedience to Jehovah's law against idolatry, they firmly made it known that they served Jehovah and that he was their Supreme Sovereign. Faithfulness to God was more precious to them than their present life!—Daniel 3:14-18.

14 Are we to conclude from such examples that to be loyal to Jehovah, a person has to be perfect or that one who makes a mistake has completely failed? By

---

13. How was the Devil proved a liar regarding (a) Job? (b) the three Hebrews?

14. How is it possible for us as imperfect humans to prove that we are truly loyal to Jehovah?

no means! The Bible tells us that at times Moses fell short. Although Jehovah was displeased, he did not reject Moses. The apostles of Jesus Christ also had their weaknesses. Taking into account our inheritance of imperfection, Jehovah is pleased if we do not *deliberately* ignore his will in any respect. If because of weakness we do become involved in wrongdoing, it is important that we sincerely repent and not make a practice of the error. In this way we demonstrate that we truly do love what Jehovah says is good and hate what he shows to be bad. On the basis of our faith in the sin-atoning value of Jesus' sacrifice, we can enjoy a clean standing before God.—Amos 5:15; Acts 3:19; Hebrews 9:14.

15 Nevertheless, could it be that *perfect* obedience to Jehovah's sovereignty is simply not possible for humans? The answer to this was like a "sacred secret" for some 4,000 years. (1 Timothy 3:16) Adam, though created perfect, did not set a perfect example of godly devotion. So who could? Certainly none of his sinful offspring. The only man to do so was Jesus Christ. (Hebrews 4:15) What Jesus accomplished proved that Adam, who had more favorable circumstances, could have maintained perfect integrity if he had wanted to. The fault was not in God's creative work. Jesus Christ is therefore the example that we seek to imitate in demonstrating not only obedience to divine law but also personal devotion to Jehovah, the Universal Sovereign.—Deuteronomy 32:4, 5.

---

15. (a) Who among all humans maintained *perfect* integrity to God, and what did this prove? (b) How are we helped by what Jesus did?

What Is Our Personal Answer?

16 Each of us today has to face the issue of universal sovereignty. If we have openly stated that we are on Jehovah's side, Satan makes us a target. He brings pressure from every direction and will continue to do so down to the end of his wicked system of things. We must not let our guard down. (1 Peter 5:8) Our conduct shows where we stand on the supreme issue of Jehovah's sovereignty and the secondary issue of integrity to God under test. We cannot afford to view disloyal conduct as unimportant simply because it is common in the world. Maintaining integrity requires that we endeavor to apply Jehovah's righteous ways in every matter of life.

17 For example, we cannot imitate Satan, who is "the father of the lie." (John 8:44) We must be truthful in all our dealings. In Satan's system, young people often are not truthful with their parents. But Christian youths avoid this, and thus they prove untrue Satan's charge that God's people would abandon their integrity under test. (Job 1:9-11; Proverbs 6:16-19) Then there are business practices that might identify a person with "the father of the lie" instead of with the God of truth. These, we shun. (Micah 6:11, 12) Too, stealing is never justified, even if a person is in need or if the one from whom items are taken is wealthy. (Proverbs 6:30, 31; 1 Peter 4:15) Even if it is a common practice where we live or if what is taken is small, stealing is still con-

---

16. Why must we be constantly on the alert as to our attitude toward Jehovah's sovereignty?
17. What is there about the origin of lying and stealing that should make us shun them?

trary to God's laws.—Luke 16:10; Romans 12:2; Ephesians 4:28.

18 During the Thousand Year Reign of Christ, Satan and his demons will be in the abyss, unable to influence mankind. What a relief that will be! But following the thousand years, they will be loosed for a little time. Satan and those who follow him will put pressure on those of restored mankind who are maintaining their integrity to God. (Revelation 20:7-10) If it is our privilege to be alive then, how will we react regarding the issue of universal sovereignty? Since all mankind will then be perfect, any act of disloyalty will be deliberate and will result in eternal destruction. How vital it is that we cultivate the habit now of responding positively to whatever direction Jehovah gives us, whether through his Word or through his organization! Doing so, we show our genuine devotion to him as the Universal Sovereign.

---

18. (a) At the end of Christ's Thousand Year Reign, what test will come on all humankind? (b) What habit should we cultivate now?

Review Discussion

- What is the great issue that we all have to face? How did we get involved?
- What is outstanding about the ways in which men and women of ancient times proved their integrity to Jehovah?
- Why is it vital that we honor Jehovah by our conduct each day?

CHAPTER SEVEN

What We Learn From God's Permission of Wickedness

"FEW and distressing the days of the years of my life have proved," said the patriarch Jacob. (Genesis 47:9) Similarly, Job stated that man "is short-lived and glutted with agitation." (Job 14:1) Like them, most of us have experienced difficulties, injustices, even tragedies. Yet, our being born was no injustice on God's part. True, we do not have the perfection of mind and body and the Paradise home that Adam and Eve originally had. But what if Jehovah had immediately executed them when they rebelled? While there would not have been any sickness, sorrow, or death, there would not have been a human race either. We would not have been born. Mercifully, God allowed Adam and Eve time to bring forth children, even though these inherited imperfection. And through Christ, Jehovah made provision for us to get back what Adam had lost—everlasting life on a paradise earth.—John 10:10; Romans 5:12.

2 How encouraging it is for us to be able to look forward to living forever in the new world amid Paradise surroundings, where we will be free from sickness, sorrow, pain, and death, as well as from wicked people!

1, 2. (a) If Jehovah had promptly executed the rebels in Eden, how would that have affected us? (b) What loving provisions has Jehovah made available to us?

(Proverbs 2:21, 22; Revelation 21:4, 5) But from the Bible record, we learn that while our personal salvation is very important to us and to Jehovah, something even more significant is involved.

For the Sake of His Great Name

3 God's name is involved in the fulfillment of his purpose regarding the earth and mankind. That name, Jehovah, means "He Causes to Become." So his name embodies his reputation as the Universal Sovereign, the Purposer, and the God of truth. Because of Jehovah's position, the peace and well-being of the entire universe require that his name and what it encompasses be given the full respect it deserves and that all be obedient to him.

4 After creating Adam and Eve, Jehovah gave them an assignment to fulfill. He made it clear that his purpose was not only to subdue all the earth—thus extending the boundaries of Paradise—but to populate it with their descendants. (Genesis 1:28) Was this purpose going to fail because of their sin? What a reproach it would be to the name of the almighty Jehovah if he could not fulfill his purpose toward this earth and humanity!

5 Jehovah had warned Adam and Eve that if they were disobedient and ate from the tree of the

---

3. What is involved in connection with the fulfillment of Jehovah's purpose for the earth and mankind?
4. What did Jehovah's purpose for the earth include?
5. (a) If the first humans ate from the tree of the knowledge of good and bad, when would they die? (b) How did Jehovah fulfill his word at Genesis 2:17 while respecting his purpose regarding the earth?

knowledge of good and bad, they would die *"in the day"* of their eating. (Genesis 2:17) True to his word, Jehovah called them to account on the very day of their sinning and pronounced the sentence of death. From God's standpoint, Adam and Eve died that day. To carry out his purpose regarding the earth, however, Jehovah allowed them to produce a family before they died physically. Nevertheless, since God can view 1,000 years as one day, when Adam's life ended at 930 years, it was within one "day." (2 Peter 3:8; Genesis 5:3-5) Thus Jehovah's truthfulness was upheld as to when punishment would be executed, and his purpose for the earth was not thwarted by their deaths. But for a time, imperfect people, including wicked ones, have been allowed to live.

6 What Jehovah said to the ruler of Egypt in the days of Moses further indicates why God has allowed the wicked to continue. When Pharaoh forbade the departure of the sons of Israel from Egypt, Jehovah did not immediately strike him down. Ten Plagues were brought on the land, demonstrating Jehovah's power in amazing ways. When warning of the seventh plague, Jehovah told Pharaoh that He could easily have wiped Pharaoh and his people off the face of the earth. "But, in fact," Jehovah said, "for this cause I have kept you in existence, for the sake of showing you my power and in order to have my name declared in all the earth."—Exodus 9:15, 16.

6, 7. (a) According to Exodus 9:15, 16, why does Jehovah allow the wicked to continue for a time? (b) In Pharaoh's case, how was Jehovah's power shown, and how was His name made known? (c) What will result when the present wicked system ends?

7 When Jehovah delivered the Israelites, his name did indeed come to be widely known. (Joshua 2:1, 9-11) Today, nearly 3,500 years later, what he did back then has not been forgotten. Not only was the personal name Jehovah declared but so was the truth about the One bearing that name. This established Jehovah's reputation as the God who keeps his promises and takes action in behalf of his servants. (Joshua 23:14) It demonstrated that because of his almighty power, nothing can block his purpose. (Isaiah 14:24, 27) We can therefore be confident that he will soon take action in behalf of his faithful servants by destroying Satan's entire wicked system. That display of almighty power and the glory it brings to Jehovah's name will never be forgotten. The benefits will be unending. —Ezekiel 38:23; Revelation 19:1, 2.

'O the Depth of God's Wisdom!'

8 In his letter to the Romans, the apostle Paul raises the question: "Is there injustice with God?" He emphatically answers: "Never may that become so!" Then he emphasizes God's mercy and refers to what Jehovah said about allowing Pharaoh to live a while longer. Paul also shows that we humans are like clay in the hands of a potter. He then states: "If, now, God, although having the will to demonstrate his wrath and to make his power known, tolerated with much long-suffering vessels of wrath made fit for destruction, in order that he might make known the riches of his glory upon vessels of mercy, which he prepared

---

8. What factors does Paul urge us to consider?

beforehand for glory, namely, us, whom he called not only from among Jews but also from among nations, what of it?"—Romans 9:14-24.

9 Ever since the rebellion in Eden, any who have opposed Jehovah and his laws have been "vessels of wrath made fit for destruction." During all the time since then, Jehovah has exercised long-suffering. The wicked have ridiculed his ways, persecuted his servants, even killed his Son. Showing great restraint, Jehovah has allowed enough time for all creation to see fully the disastrous results of rebellion against God and of human rule independent of him. At the same time, Jesus' death provided the means for delivering obedient mankind and for 'breaking up the works of the Devil.' —1 John 3:8; Hebrews 2:14, 15.

10 During the more than 1,900 years since Jesus' resurrection, Jehovah has tolerated further the "vessels of wrath," holding off their destruction. Why? For one thing, because he has been preparing those who are to be associated with Jesus Christ in his heavenly Kingdom. These are 144,000 in number, and they are the "vessels of mercy" spoken of by the apostle Paul. First, individuals from among the Jews were invited to make up this heavenly class. Later, God invited people of the Gentile nations. Jehovah has not forced any of these to

---

9. (a) Who are the "vessels of wrath made fit for destruction"? (b) Why has Jehovah shown great long-suffering in the face of his opposers, and how will the final outcome be for the good of those who love him?

10. Why has Jehovah tolerated the wicked for the past 1,900 years?

serve him. But from among those who responded appreciatively to his loving provisions, he gave some the privilege of being corulers with his Son in the heavenly Kingdom. The preparation of that heavenly class is now nearly complete.—Luke 22:29; Revelation 14:1-4.

11 But what about inhabitants for the earth? Jehovah's long-suffering has also made possible the gathering together of "a great crowd" out of all nations. They now number into the millions. Jehovah has promised that this earthly class will survive the end of this system and have the prospect of everlasting life on a paradise earth. (Revelation 7:9, 10; Psalm 37:29; John 10:16) In God's due time, multitudes of the dead will be resurrected and given the opportunity to be earthly subjects of the heavenly Kingdom. God's Word foretells at Acts 24:15: "There is going to be a resurrection of both the righteous and the unrighteous." —John 5:28, 29.

12 Has there been any injustice in all of this? No, because by holding off his destruction of the wicked, or "vessels of wrath," God is showing compassion to others, in harmony with his purpose. This shows how merciful and loving he is. Too, having had time to observe the unfolding of his purpose, we learn much about Jehovah himself. We marvel at the various aspects of his personality that come to light—his

---

11. (a) What group is now benefiting from Jehovah's long-suffering? (b) How will the dead benefit?

12. (a) What have we learned about Jehovah from his toleration of wickedness? (b) How do you feel about how Jehovah has handled these matters?

justice, his mercy, his long-suffering, his diversified wisdom. Jehovah's wise handling of the issue of universal sovereignty—his right to rule—will forever stand as a testimony to the fact that his way of ruling is the very best. With the apostle Paul, we say: "O the depth of God's riches and wisdom and knowledge! How unsearchable his judgments are and past tracing out his ways are!"—Romans 11:33.

Opportunity to Show Our Devotion

13 Many of God's servants are in situations that involve personal suffering. Their suffering continues because God has not yet destroyed the wicked and brought about the foretold restoration of mankind. Should this embitter us? Or can we see such situations as opportunities to have a share in proving the Devil a liar? We can be strengthened to do so if we keep in mind the appeal: "Be wise, my son, and make my heart rejoice, that I may make a reply to him that is taunting me." (Proverbs 27:11) Satan, the one who taunts Jehovah, charged that if people suffer material loss or physical affliction, they will blame God, even curse him. (Job 1:9-11; 2:4, 5) We bring joy to Jehovah's heart when, by our loyalty to him in the face of hardships, we show that such is not true in our case.

14 If we rely on Jehovah when we undergo trials, we can develop precious qualities. For example, as a result of the things that Jesus suffered, he "learned obe-

---

13. When we experience personal suffering, what opportunity is presented to us, and what will help us to respond wisely?
14. If we rely on Jehovah when we undergo trials, what benefits can come to us?

dience" in a way that he had never known it before. We too can learn from our trials in that we can cultivate long-suffering, endurance, and a deepened appreciation of Jehovah's righteous ways.—Hebrews 5:8, 9; 12:11; James 1:2-4.

15 Others will observe what we do. Because of what we undergo on account of our love for righteousness, some of them may in time come to appreciate who the true Christians are today. And by uniting with us in worship, they can come in line for the blessings

15. As we patiently endure hardship, how may others benefit?

Jehovah "blessed the end of Job afterward more than his beginning"

of everlasting life. (Matthew 25:34-36, 40, 46) Jehovah and his Son want people to have that opportunity.

16 How fine it is when we view even difficult situations as opportunities to show our devotion to Jehovah as well as to share in accomplishing his will! Our doing so can give evidence that we are indeed moving toward unity with God and Christ. Jesus prayed to Jehovah in behalf of all true Christians, saying: "I make request, not concerning these [his immediate disciples] only, but also concerning those putting faith in me through their word; in order that they may all be one, just as you, Father, are in union with me and I am in union with you, that they also may be in union with us."—John 17:20, 21.

17 If we are loyal to Jehovah, he will reward us generously. His Word says: "Become steadfast, unmovable, always having plenty to do in the work of the Lord, knowing that your labor is not in vain in connection with the Lord." (1 Corinthians 15:58) It also states: "God is not unrighteous so as to forget your work and the love you showed for his name." (Hebrews 6:10) James 5:11 notes: "Look! We pronounce happy those who have endured. You have heard of the endurance of Job and have seen the outcome Jehovah gave, that Jehovah is very tender in affection and merciful." What was the outcome for Job? "As for Jehovah, he blessed the end of Job afterward more than his beginning." (Job 42:10-16) Yes, Jehovah is "the rewarder of those earnestly seeking him." (Hebrews 11:6) And

---

16. How is our view of personal hardship related to the matter of unity?
17. What confidence can we have if we are loyal to Jehovah?

what a reward we have to look forward to—everlasting life on a paradise earth!

18 God's Kingdom rule will undo all the damage done to the human family for the past thousands of years. The joys at that time will far outweigh any suffering that we experience now. We will not be disturbed by any bad memories of previous suffering. The upbuilding thoughts and activities that will fill the everyday life of people in the new world will gradually erase the painful memories. Jehovah declares: "I am creating new heavens [a new heavenly Kingdom government over mankind] and a new earth [a righteous human society]; and the former things will not be called to mind, neither will they come up into the heart. But exult, you people, and be joyful forever in what I am creating." Yes, in Jehovah's new world, righteous ones will be able to say: "The whole earth has come to rest, has become free of disturbance. People have become cheerful with joyful cries."—Isaiah 14:7; 65:17, 18.

---

18. What will eventually happen to any painful memories we may have?

Review Discussion

- While permitting evil, how has Jehovah properly shown great respect for his own name?
- How has God's tolerating "vessels of wrath" enabled his mercy to reach all the way to us?
- What should we endeavor to see in situations that involve personal suffering?

CHAPTER EIGHT

'Wrestling Against Wicked Spirit Forces'

MANY people scoff at the idea that there are wicked spirits. But it is no laughing matter. Whether people believe it or not, wicked spirits do exist, and they try to exert pressure on everyone. Worshipers of Jehovah are not exempt. In fact, they are the primary target. The apostle Paul alerts us to that fact, saying: "We have a wrestling, not against blood and flesh, but against the [invisible] governments, against the authorities, against the world rulers of this darkness, against the wicked spirit forces in the heavenly places." (Ephesians 6:12) In our day the pressure exerted by wicked spirit forces has reached an all-time high because Satan has been cast out of heaven and is furious, knowing that his time is short.—Revelation 12:12.

2 Is it possible to win a struggle against superhuman spirit forces? Yes, but only by complete reliance on Jehovah. We must listen to him and obey his Word. By so doing, we can be spared much of the physical, moral, and emotional damage experienced by those under satanic control.—James 4:7.

---

1. Why is the activity of wicked spirits of particular interest to us?

2. How is it possible for us to win in the struggle against superhuman spirits?

World Rulers in Heavenly Places

3 Jehovah vividly describes for us the world situation as he sees it from his vantage point in the heavens. He gave the apostle John a vision in which Satan was depicted as "a great fiery-colored dragon." He was poised to devour, if possible, God's Messianic Kingdom as soon as it was brought to birth in heaven in 1914. Failing in that, Satan unleashed a flood of vicious opposition against the earthly representatives of that Kingdom. (Revelation 12:3, 4, 13, 17) How would Satan wage this warfare? Through his own human representatives.

4 John was next shown a wild beast with seven heads and ten horns, a beast having authority "over every tribe and people and tongue and nation." That beast represents the entire global political system. John was informed that "the dragon [Satan the Devil] gave to the beast its power and its throne and great authority." (Revelation 13:1, 2, 7) Yes, Satan is the source of the power and authority of human governments. Thus, as the apostle Paul wrote, the true "world rulers" are "wicked spirit forces in the heavenly places," who control human governments. All who would worship Jehovah need to grasp the full significance of that. —Luke 4:5, 6.

5 Although many political rulers profess to be religious, none of the nations submit to Jehovah's rulership or to that of his appointed King, Jesus Christ. All

---

3. Whom does Satan viciously oppose, and how?
4. Who is the source of the power of human governments, and how do we know that?
5. To what are political rulers now being gathered?

struggle fiercely to hold on to their own power. Today, as the account in Revelation shows, "expressions inspired by demons" are gathering the world's rulers to "the war of the great day of God the Almighty" at Armageddon.—Revelation 16:13, 14, 16; 19:17-19.

6 Every day, people's lives are touched by political, social, economic, and religious conflicts that tear the human family apart. In these conflicts, it is common for people to take sides—verbally or otherwise—with the nation, tribe, language group, or social class of which they are a part. Even when people are not directly involved in some conflict, they often find themselves favoring one side over another. But regardless of which person or cause they endorse, to whom are they really giving support? The Bible plainly states: "The whole world is lying in the power of the wicked one." (1 John 5:19) How, then, can a person avoid being misled with the rest of mankind? Only by giving his full support to God's Kingdom and by maintaining complete neutrality as to conflicts of the world.—John 17:15, 16.

Sly Devices of the Wicked One

7 In all periods of history, Satan has used verbal and physical persecution to turn individuals away from true worship. He has also employed more subtle means—cunning acts and sly devices. He has cleverly kept a large proportion of mankind in darkness by means of false religion, making them think that they are serving God. Lacking in accurate knowledge of God and in love for truth, they may be at-

---

6. Why is care needed in order to avoid being maneuvered into giving support to the satanic system?
7. How is Satan's cleverness shown in his use of false religion?

tracted by mystical and emotional religious services or be impressed by powerful works. (2 Thessalonians 2: 9, 10) But we are warned that even from among those who once shared in true worship, "some will fall away . . . , paying attention to misleading inspired utterances and teachings of demons." (1 Timothy 4:1) How could that happen?

8 Slyly, the Devil plays on our weaknesses. Does fear of man still have a hold on us? If so, we may give in to pressure from relatives or neighbors to share in practices that are of false religious origin. Are we proud? If so, we may take offense when counseled or when others do not accept ideas that we advocate. (Proverbs 15: 10; 29:25; 1 Timothy 6:3, 4) Instead of adjusting our viewpoint to conform to the example of Christ, we may incline toward those who 'tickle our ears' by saying that just reading the Bible and living a good life are enough. (2 Timothy 4:3) Whether we actually join another religious group or simply hold to our own brand of religion is not important to Satan, just as long as we do not worship Jehovah in the way that God directs through his Word and his organization.

9 Satan also cunningly entices people to satisfy normal desires in wrong ways. He has done this with the desire for sexual intimacies. Rejecting Bible morality, many in the world view sexual relations between unmarried people as legitimate pleasure or as a way of proving that they are adults. And what about those who are married? Many commit adultery.

---

8. How can Satan lure us into false religion even if we are worshiping Jehovah?
9. How does Satan cunningly use sex to accomplish his aims?

And even when there is no infidelity in their marriage, numerous individuals seek a divorce or separation so that they can take up living with someone else. Satan's subtle approach aims to influence people to live for pleasure *now,* inducing them to ignore the long-range effects not only on themselves and others but especially on their relationship with Jehovah and his Son. —1 Corinthians 6:9, 10; Galatians 6:7, 8.

10 Another natural desire is for recreation. When wholesome, it can be physically, mentally, and emotionally refreshing. But how do we react when Satan cleverly uses occasions of relaxation to try to alienate our thinking from God's? We know, for example, that Jehovah hates sexual immorality and violence. When movies, television programs, or theater performances feature those things, do we passively sit and take it all in? Keep in mind, too, that Satan will see to it that such things become more debased as the time for his destruction nears, since "wicked men and impostors will advance from bad to worse, misleading and being misled." (2 Timothy 3:13) So we constantly need to be on guard against Satan's designs.—Genesis 6:13; Psalm 11:5; Romans 1:24-32.

11 We are also aware that those who indulge in any form of spiritism—practicing divination, employing witchcraft, or trying to communicate with the dead—are detestable to Jehovah. (Deuteronomy 18:10-12) Bearing that in mind, we would not think of con-

---

10. By what means does Satan try to subvert our attitude toward immorality and violence?
11. In what ways might even a person who knows the truth about spiritism be ensnared if he is not alert?

sulting spirit mediums, and we would certainly not welcome them into our home to practice their demonic arts. But would we listen to them if they appeared on our television screen or on the Internet? Although we would never accept treatment from a witch doctor, might we tie a string around the wrist of our newborn, with the thought that it might somehow protect the child from harm? Knowing that the Bible condemns binding others with a spell, would we allow a hypnotist to take control of our mind?—Galatians 5:19-21.

12 The Bible says that fornication and uncleanness of every sort should not (with unclean motives) even be mentioned among us. (Ephesians 5:3-5) But what if such themes are accompanied by music that has a pleasing melody, a catchy rhythm, or a persistent beat? Will we start to repeat lyrics that glorify sex without marriage, the use of drugs for pleasure, and other sinful acts? Or while we know that we should not imitate the way of life of people who indulge in such things, do we tend to identify ourselves with them by imitating the way they dress, their hairstyles, or their way of speaking? How insidious the methods are that Satan uses to entice humans to conform to his own corrupted way of thinking! (2 Corinthians 4:3, 4) To keep from falling victim to his sly devices, we must avoid drifting along with the world. We need to keep in mind who "the world rulers of this darkness" are and earnestly wrestle against their influence.—1 Peter 5:8.

---

12. (a) How is music used to get us to think about ideas that we know are wrong? (b) How might a person's clothing, hairstyle, or manner of speech indicate admiration for those whose life-style Jehovah disapproves? (c) What is required on our part if we are to avoid falling victim to Satan's sly devices?

Equipped to Be Conquerors

13 Before his death, Jesus said to his apostles: "Take courage! I have conquered the world." (John 16:33) They too could be conquerors. Some 60 years later, the apostle John wrote: "Who is the one that conquers the world but he who has faith that Jesus is the Son of God?" (1 John 5:5) Such faith is shown by our obeying Jesus' commands and relying on God's Word, even as Jesus did. What else is required? That we stay close to the congregation of which he is Head. When we fall short, we must earnestly repent and seek God's forgiveness on the basis of Jesus' sacrifice. In this way, despite our imperfections and mistakes, we too can be conquerors.—Psalm 130:3, 4.

---

13. How is it possible for any of us, with our imperfections, to conquer the world that Satan rules?

The nations are being gathered to Armageddon

14 To succeed, we need to put on "the complete suit of armor from God," neglecting no part of it. Please open your Bible to Ephesians 6:13-17, and read its description of that armor. Then, by answering the questions below, consider how you can benefit from the protection afforded by each piece of armor.

"Loins girded about with truth"

Even though we may know the truth, how do regular study, meditation on Bible truth, and meeting attendance protect us? (1 Corinthians 10:12, 13; 2 Corinthians 13:5; Philippians 4:8, 9)

"Breastplate of righteousness"

Whose standard of righteousness is this? (Revelation 15:3)

Illustrate how failure to follow Jehovah's righteous ways exposes one to spiritual harm. (Deuteronomy 7:3, 4; 1 Samuel 15:22, 23)

"Feet shod with the equipment of the good news of peace"

How is it a safeguard for us to keep our feet busy taking us to talk to people about God's provisions for peace? (Psalm 73:2, 3; Romans 10:15; 1 Timothy 5:13)

"Large shield of faith"

If we have faith that is firmly founded, how will we react in the face of efforts that are meant to cause us to doubt or fear? (2 Kings 6:15-17; 2 Timothy 1:12)

---

14. Read Ephesians 6:13-17, and use the questions and scriptures provided in this paragraph as a basis for discussing benefits from each part of the spiritual armor.

"Helmet of salvation"

How does the hope of salvation help one to avoid being ensnared by excessive concern with material possessions? (1 Timothy 6:7-10, 19)

"Sword of the spirit"

On what should we always rely when fighting off onslaughts against our spirituality or that of others? (Psalm 119:98; Proverbs 3:5, 6; Matthew 4:3, 4)

What else is vital to success in spiritual warfare? How often is it to be employed? In behalf of whom? (Ephesians 6:18, 19)

15 As soldiers of Christ, we are part of a large army engaging in spiritual warfare. If we keep alert and make good use of the full suit of armor from God, we will not become casualties in this war. Instead, we will be a strengthening help to fellow servants of God. We will be ready and eager to take the offensive, spreading the good news of God's Messianic Kingdom, the heavenly government that Satan so violently opposes.

---

15. How can we take the offensive in the spiritual fight?

Review Discussion

- Why do worshipers of Jehovah maintain complete neutrality as to the world's conflicts?
- What are some of the sly devices used by Satan to bring Christians to spiritual ruin?
- How does the spiritual armor provided by God safeguard us in our spiritual warfare?

CHAPTER NINE

The Power of the Resurrection Hope

HAVE you lost loved ones in death? Without the resurrection, there would be no hope of ever seeing them again. They would remain in the condition that the Bible describes when it states: "As for the dead, they are conscious of nothing at all, . . . for there is no work nor devising nor knowledge nor wisdom in Sheol [the grave], the place to which you are going."—Ecclesiastes 9:5, 10.

2 Mercifully, by means of the resurrection, Jehovah has opened up the priceless opportunity for untold multitudes of people who have died to come back from the dead and enjoy eternal life. This means that you can have the heartwarming hope that someday, in God's new world, you will be reunited with loved ones who have fallen asleep in death.—Mark 5:35, 41, 42; Acts 9:36-41.

3 Because of the resurrection, we do not need to have a morbid fear of death. Jehovah can, without

---

1. Without the resurrection hope, what prospect would the dead have?

2. What marvelous prospect is made possible by the resurrection?

3. (a) In what ways has the resurrection proved to be important in the carrying out of Jehovah's purpose? (b) When in particular is the resurrection hope a source of strength to us?

lasting harm to his faithful servants, let Satan go to the limit in trying to prove his malicious charge that "everything that a man has he will give in behalf of his soul." (Job 2:4) Jesus was faithful to God even to death, and therefore God resurrected him to heavenly life. Thus, Jesus was able to present the value of his perfect human sacrifice before his Father's heavenly throne, with lifesaving benefit to us. By means of the resurrection, those of the "little flock," as joint heirs with Christ, have the hope of being united with him in the heavenly Kingdom. (Luke 12:32) For others, there is the hope of a resurrection to everlasting life on a paradise earth. (Psalm 37:11, 29) All Christians find the resurrection hope to be a source of strength "beyond what is normal" when they undergo trials that bring them face-to-face with death.—2 Corinthians 4:7.

Why Fundamental to Christian Faith

4 The resurrection is, as stated at Hebrews 6:1, 2, a "primary doctrine." It is part of the foundation of faith without which we could never become mature Christians. (1 Corinthians 15:16-19) However, the Bible's teaching of the resurrection is alien to the thinking of the world in general. Lacking spirituality, more and more people see only this life as real. Thus, they live in pursuit of pleasure. Then there are those adherents of traditional religions—both inside and outside of Christendom—who think that they have an

4. (a) In what sense is the resurrection a "primary doctrine"? (b) What does the resurrection mean to the world in general?

immortal soul. But that belief cannot be reconciled with the Bible's teaching of a resurrection, since a resurrection would be unnecessary if humans had an immortal soul. Trying to merge these two concepts is more confusing than hope-inspiring. How can we help honesthearted ones who want to know the truth?

5 Before such ones can appreciate what a wonderful provision the resurrection is, they need to have the correct understanding about the soul and the condition of the dead. Often, just a few scriptures are sufficient to make these matters clear to a person who is hungry for Bible truth. (Genesis 2:7; Psalm 146:3, 4; Ezekiel 18:4) However, some modern translations and paraphrase editions of the Bible obscure the truth about the soul. So it may be necessary to consider the expressions used in the Bible's original languages.

6 The *New World Translation* is especially valuable in doing this because it consistently renders the Hebrew term *ne′phesh* and the corresponding Greek word *psy-khe′* as "soul." In the appendix of this translation are listed many texts where these terms are found. Many other Bible versions are not consistent but may render the same original words not only as "soul" but also as "creature," "being," "person," and "life"; "my *ne′phesh*" may be rendered "I," and "your *ne′phesh,*"

---

5. (a) Before a person can appreciate the resurrection, what does he need to know? (b) What scriptures would you use to explain the soul? the condition of the dead? (c) What may be done if someone uses a Bible translation that seems to obscure the truth?
6. How could you help a person understand what the soul is?

"you." A comparison of other Bible translations with the *New World Translation* will help a sincere student to appreciate that the original-language terms rendered "soul" refer both to people and to animals. But never do these terms convey the idea that a soul is an invisible, intangible thing that can escape from the body at death and have continued conscious existence somewhere.

7 The *New World Translation* is also consistent in using the word "Sheol" to transliterate the Hebrew term *she'ohl'* and in its use of "Hades" for the Greek term *hai'des* and "Gehenna" for the Greek term *ge'en·na.* "Sheol" is the equivalent of the word "Hades." (Psalm 16:10; Acts 2:27) The Bible makes it clear that both Sheol and Hades refer to mankind's common grave and are associated with death, not life. (Psalm 89:48; Revelation 20:13) The Scriptures also point to the prospect of return from the common grave by means of a resurrection. (Job 14:13; Acts 2:31) In contrast, no hope of future life is held out for those who go to Gehenna, and the soul is never spoken of as having conscious existence there.—Matthew 10:28.

8 With those matters cleared up, a person can then be helped to grasp what the resurrection might mean to him. He can begin to appreciate Jehovah's love in making such a marvelous provision. The grief felt by those who have lost dear ones in death can be soft-

---

7. How would you explain from the Bible the condition of those in Sheol? in Hades? in Gehenna?

8. How can properly understanding the resurrection influence a person's attitude and actions?

ened by the joyful anticipation of reunion in God's new world. Understanding these matters is also the key to understanding the meaning of the death of Christ. First-century Christians realized that the resurrection of Jesus Christ is fundamental to the Christian faith, opening the way for the resurrection of others. They zealously preached about Jesus' resurrection and the hope that it gives. So, too, those today who appreciate the resurrection are eager to share this precious truth with others.—Acts 5:30-32; 10:42, 43.

Using 'the Key of Hades'

9 All who are to be associated with Christ in his heavenly Kingdom must eventually die. But they well know the assurance that he gave when he said: "I became dead, but, look! I am living forever and ever, and I have the keys of death and of Hades." (Revelation 1: 18) What did he mean? He was calling attention to his own experience. He too had died. But God did not leave him in Hades. On the third day, Jehovah personally raised him to spirit life and conferred immortality upon him. (Acts 2:32, 33; 10:40) In addition, God gave him "the keys of death and of Hades" to use in releasing others from mankind's common grave and from the effects of Adamic sin. Because he possesses those keys, Jesus is able to raise his faithful followers from the dead. He resurrects the spirit-anointed members of his congregation first, giving them the precious gift of immortal life in heaven, just as his Father gave him.—Romans 6:5; Philippians 3:20, 21.

---

9. How does Jesus first use "the keys of death and of Hades"?

10 When would faithful anointed Christians experience that heavenly resurrection? The Bible indicates that it has already begun. The apostle Paul explained that they would be raised 'during Christ's presence,' which presence began in the year 1914. (1 Corinthians 15:23) When anointed faithful ones finish their earthly course now during his presence, they do not have to remain in death until the return of their Lord. As soon as they die, they are raised up in the spirit, being "changed, in a moment, in the twinkling of an eye." What happiness is theirs, since the good works they did "go right with them"!—1 Corinthians 15:51, 52; Revelation 14:13.

---

10. When does the resurrection of faithful anointed Christians take place?

11 But the resurrection of Kingdom heirs to heavenly life is not the only resurrection. The fact that it is called "the first resurrection" at Revelation 20:6 indicates that another must follow. Those who benefit from this latter resurrection will have the happy prospect of everlasting life on a paradise earth. When will that take place? The book of Revelation shows that it will be after "the earth and the heaven"—the present wicked system of things, with its ruling authorities—are removed. That end of the old system is very near. Thereafter, at God's appointed time, the earthly resurrection will begin.—Revelation 20:11, 12.

---

11. What resurrection will there be for people in general, and when will it begin?

Jehovah promises that there is going to be a resurrection of both the righteous and the unrighteous

12 Who will be included in that earthly resurrection? Among them will be faithful servants of Jehovah from earliest times, men and women who because of their strong faith in the resurrection "would not accept release by some ransom." That is, they would not compromise their integrity to God in order to escape a violent, premature death. What a delight it will be to get to know them personally and to hear from them firsthand the details concerning events that are reported on only briefly in the Bible! Also resurrected to earthly life will be Abel, the first faithful witness of Jehovah; Enoch and Noah, fearless proclaimers of God's message of warning before the Deluge; Abraham and Sarah, who entertained angels; Moses, through whom the Law was given at Mount Sinai; courageous prophets such as Jeremiah, who saw the destruction of Jerusalem in 607 B.C.E.; and John the Baptizer, who heard God himself identify Jesus as His Son. In addition, there will be many loyal men and women who died during these last days of this present wicked system of things.—Hebrews 11:4-38; Matthew 11:11.

13 In time, others besides faithful servants of God will also be raised from the dead, leaving no one in the common grave of mankind. The extent to which that grave is emptied of its dead can be seen in the use that Jesus will make of 'the key of Hades' in behalf of

---

12. Who will be included among the faithful ones raised to life on earth, and why is that a thrilling prospect?

13, 14. (a) What will happen to Hades and the dead therein? (b) Who will be included in the resurrection, and why?

mankind. This is shown in a vision given to the apostle John, in which he saw Hades "hurled into the lake of fire." (Revelation 20:14) What does that mean? It means that Hades, the common grave of mankind, is totally destroyed. It goes out of existence, being completely emptied of its dead, because in addition to resurrecting all faithful worshipers of Jehovah, Jesus will also mercifully bring back even unrighteous ones. God's Word assures us: "There is going to be a resurrection of both the righteous and the unrighteous." —Acts 24:15.

14 None of these unrighteous ones are raised simply to be judged worthy of death again. In the righteous environment that will prevail earth wide under God's Kingdom, they will be helped to bring their lives into harmony with Jehovah's ways. The vision showed that "the scroll of life" will be opened. Hence, they will have opportunity to get their names entered in it. They will be "judged individually according to their deeds" performed *after* their resurrection. (Revelation 20:12, 13) Thus, viewed from the standpoint of the final outcome, theirs can prove to be "a resurrection of life" and will not unavoidably be "a resurrection of [condemnatory] judgment."—John 5:28, 29.

15 However, not all who have ever lived and died will be resurrected. Some committed sins for which no forgiveness is possible. Such ones are, not in Hades, but in Gehenna, where they experience everlasting

15. (a) Who will not be resurrected? (b) How should knowledge of the truth about the resurrection affect us?

destruction. Included among these will also be those executed in the "great tribulation," now near. (Matthew 12:31, 32; 23:33; 24:21, 22; 25:41, 46; 2 Thessalonians 1:6-9) Thus, while extraordinary mercy is shown by Jehovah in releasing the dead from Hades, the resurrection hope provides no basis for our being indifferent about how we live now. No resurrection is possible for those who willfully rebel against Jehovah's sovereignty. This knowledge should motivate us to show that we deeply appreciate the undeserved kindness of God by living our lives according to his will.

Strengthened by the Resurrection Hope

16 Those of us who have made the resurrection hope our own are able to draw great strength from it. At present, when we near the end of our life, we know that we cannot indefinitely postpone death—regardless of the medical procedures used. (Ecclesiastes 8:8) If we have loyally served Jehovah with his organization, we can look to the future with full confidence. We know that by means of the resurrection, we will enjoy life again, in God's due time. And what a life it will be! "The real life," as the apostle Paul called it. —1 Timothy 6:19; Hebrews 6:10-12.

17 Knowing that there is a resurrection and knowing the One who is the source of that provision enables us to be strong in the faith. This fortifies us to be loyal to God even if threatened with death at the hands

---

16. How can the resurrection hope be a source of great strength?
17. What can help us maintain integrity to Jehovah?

of violent persecutors. Satan has long used fear of untimely death as a means of holding people in slavery. But Jesus did not have such fear. He proved faithful to Jehovah right down to death. Through his ransom sacrifice, Jesus provided the means for freeing others from such fear.—Hebrews 2:14, 15.

18 As a result of their faith both in the provision of Christ's sacrifice and in the resurrection, Jehovah's servants have built up an outstanding record as integrity keepers. When put under pressure, they have proved that 'they do not love their own souls' more than they love Jehovah. (Revelation 12:11) Wisely, they do not abandon Christian principles trying to save their present life. (Luke 9:24, 25) They know that even if they lose their life now because of loyally upholding Jehovah's sovereignty, he will reward them by means of the resurrection. Do you have that kind of faith? You will if you truly love Jehovah and if you take to heart what the resurrection hope really means.

---

18. What has helped Jehovah's servants to build up such an outstanding record of integrity?

Review Discussion

- Why does a person need to have understanding regarding the soul and the condition of the dead before he can appreciate the resurrection?
- Who will return from the dead, and how should this knowledge affect us?
- How does the resurrection hope strengthen us?

CHAPTER TEN

A Kingdom "That Will Never Be Brought to Ruin"

WORLD events each day underscore the fact that humans have not found happiness by rejecting Jehovah's sovereignty and trying to govern themselves. No system of human government has brought impartial benefits to mankind. Although men have developed their scientific knowledge to an unprecedented extent, they have not been able to conquer sickness or put an end to death, not even for one individual. Human rule has not eliminated war, violence, crime, corruption, or poverty. Oppressive governments still dominate the people in many lands. (Ecclesiastes 8:9) Technology, greed, and ignorance combine to pollute the land, water, and air. Economic mismanagement by officials makes it hard for many to obtain the necessities of life. Thousands of years of human rule have made this fact obvious: "To earthling man his way does not belong. It does not belong to man who is walking even to direct his step."—Jeremiah 10:23.

2 What is the solution? God's Kingdom, for which Jesus taught his followers to pray: "Let your kingdom come. Let your will take place, as in heaven, also upon earth." (Matthew 6:9, 10) God's heavenly Kingdom is

---

1. What fact has been emphasized by world events throughout mankind's history?
2. What is the only solution to mankind's problems?

described at 2 Peter 3:13 as the "new heavens," which is to rule over the "new earth," that is, righteous human society. So important is God's heavenly Kingdom that Jesus made it the focus of his preaching. (Matthew 4:17) He showed the place that it should have in our lives, urging: "Keep on, then, seeking first the kingdom and his righteousness."—Matthew 6:33.

3 Learning about God's Kingdom is of the greatest urgency now, as soon that Kingdom will take action to change forever the rulership of this earth. Daniel 2:44 foretells: "In the days of those kings [governments now ruling] the God of heaven will set up a kingdom [in heaven] that will never be brought to ruin. And the kingdom itself will not be passed on to any other people [humans will never again rule the earth]. It will crush and put an end to all these [present] kingdoms, and it itself will stand to times indefinite." Thus the Kingdom will bring these last days to a close by destroying this entire wicked system of things. Rulership of the earth by the heavenly Kingdom will then be undisputed. How grateful we should be that the relief this will bring is now very near!

4 In 1914, Christ Jesus was installed as King and was authorized to "go subduing in the midst of [his] enemies." (Psalm 110:1, 2) Also in that year, "the last days" of this present wicked system of things began. (2 Timothy 3:1-5, 13) At the same time, events

---

3. Why is learning about God's Kingdom of the greatest urgency now?

4. In connection with the Kingdom, what took place in heaven in 1914, and why is that important to us?

that Daniel had seen in prophetic vision actually took place in heaven. "The Ancient of Days," Jehovah God, conferred upon the Son of man, Jesus Christ, "rulership and dignity and kingdom, that the peoples, national groups and languages should all serve even him." Reporting on the vision, Daniel wrote: "His rulership is an indefinitely lasting rulership that will not pass away, and his kingdom one that will not be brought to ruin." (Daniel 7:13, 14) It is by means of this heavenly Kingdom in the hands of Christ Jesus that God will enable lovers of righteousness to enjoy the countless good things that he purposed when he put our first human parents in Paradise.

5 Is it your desire to be a loyal subject of the Kingdom? If so, you will be keenly interested in the structure and operation of this heavenly government. You

5. What details regarding the Kingdom are of keen interest to us, and why?

will want to know what it is doing now, what it will accomplish in the future, and what it requires of you. As you examine the Kingdom closely, your appreciation for it should grow. If you respond to its rulership, you will be better equipped to tell others about the wonderful things God's Kingdom will do for obedient mankind.—Psalm 48:12, 13.

The Rulers of God's Kingdom

6 One of the first things such an examination reveals is that this Messianic Kingdom is an expression of Jehovah's own sovereignty. It was Jehovah who gave "rulership and dignity and kingdom" to his Son. After God's Son was empowered to begin ruling as King,

---

6. (a) How do the Scriptures show whose sovereignty is expressed by means of the Messianic Kingdom? (b) How should we be affected by what we learn about the Kingdom?

Under God's Kingdom, all people will learn righteousness

voices in heaven appropriately declared: "The kingdom of the world did become the kingdom of our Lord [Jehovah God] and of his Christ, and he [Jehovah] will rule as king forever and ever." (Revelation 11:15) So everything that we observe about this Kingdom and what it accomplishes can draw us closer to Jehovah himself. What we learn should instill in us a desire to submit to his sovereignty forever.

7 Consider, too, the fact that Jehovah has put Jesus Christ on the throne as his Deputy Ruler. As the Master Worker whom God used to make the earth and humans, Jesus knows our needs better than any of us do. Furthermore, from the beginning of human history, he demonstrated his 'fondness for the sons of men.' (Proverbs 8:30, 31; Colossians 1:15-17) So great is his love for humans that he personally came to earth and gave his life as a ransom in our behalf. (John 3:16) Thus he made available for us the means of release from sin and death and the opportunity for eternal life.—Matthew 20:28.

8 God's Kingdom is a stable, enduring government. Its enduring quality is ensured by the fact that Jehovah himself is not subject to death. (Habakkuk 1:12) In contrast with human kings, Jesus Christ, the one to whom God has entrusted kingship, is also immortal. (Romans 6:9; 1 Timothy 6:15, 16) Associated with

---

7. Why is it of special interest to us that Jesus Christ is Jehovah's Deputy Ruler?

8. (a) In contrast with human rulerships, why will God's government endure? (b) What relationship does "the faithful and discreet slave" have with the heavenly government?

Christ on heavenly thrones will be 144,000 others, loyal servants of God out of "every tribe and tongue and people and nation." These too are given immortal life. (Revelation 5:9, 10; 14:1-4; 1 Corinthians 15:42-44, 53) The vast majority of them are already in the heavens, and the remnant of them yet on earth make up the present-day "faithful and discreet slave," which loyally furthers the interests of that Kingdom here.—Matthew 24:45-47.

9 Soon now, at his appointed time, Jehovah will send his executional forces into action to cleanse the earth. They will destroy forever those humans who of their own choice refuse to acknowledge his sovereignty and who treat with scorn the loving provisions that he makes through Jesus Christ. (2 Thessalonians 1: 6-9) That will be Jehovah's day, the long-awaited time for his vindication as Universal Sovereign. "Look! The day of Jehovah itself is coming, cruel both with fury and with burning anger, . . . that it may annihilate the land's sinners out of it." (Isaiah 13:9) "That day is a day of fury, a day of distress and of anguish, a day of storm and of desolation, a day of darkness and of gloominess, a day of clouds and of thick gloom." —Zephaniah 1:15.

10 All false religion and all human governments and their armies, which have been manipulated by the unseen wicked ruler of this world, will be annihilated forever. All who identify themselves with this world by

---

9, 10. (a) What divisive, corrupting influences will the Kingdom remove? (b) If we do not want to become enemies of God's Kingdom, what entanglements should we avoid?

pursuing a self-centered, dishonest, immoral way of life will be cut off in death. Satan and his demons will be removed from contact with earth's inhabitants, securely confined for a thousand years. God's Kingdom will then have complete control of all earth's affairs. What a relief that will be for all who love righteousness!—Revelation 18:21, 24; 19:11-16, 19-21; 20:1, 2.

The Kingdom's Objectives—How Attained

11 The Messianic Kingdom will fully accomplish God's original purpose for the earth. (Genesis 1:28; 2: 8, 9, 15) To this day, mankind has failed to support that purpose. However, "the inhabited earth to come" will be subjected to the Son of man, Jesus Christ. All who survive the execution of Jehovah's judgment on this old system will work unitedly under Christ the King, gladly doing whatever he directs, so that the earth becomes a global paradise. (Hebrews 2:5-9) All mankind will enjoy the work of their hands and benefit fully from the abundance of earth's produce. —Psalm 72:1, 7, 8, 16-19; Isaiah 65:21, 22.

12 When Adam and Eve were created, they were perfect, and it was God's purpose for the earth to be filled with their offspring, all enjoying perfection in mind and body. That purpose will come to glorious reality under the rule of the Kingdom. This requires the removal of all the effects of sin, and to that end, Christ

---

11. (a) How will the Messianic Kingdom accomplish Jehovah's purpose for the earth? (b) What will Kingdom rule mean for people living on earth then?
12. How will perfection in mind and body be brought about for subjects of the Kingdom?

serves not only as King but also as High Priest. Patiently, he will help his obedient subjects to benefit from the sin-atoning value of the sacrifice of his own human life.

13 Under Kingdom rule, earth's inhabitants will realize marvelous physical benefits. "At that time the eyes of the blind ones will be opened, and the very ears of the deaf ones will be unstopped. At that time the lame one will climb up just as a stag does, and the tongue of the speechless one will cry out in gladness." (Isaiah 35:5, 6) Flesh disfigured by age or disease will become fresher than that of a child, and chronic weaknesses will give way to vigorous health. "Let his flesh become fresher than in youth; let him return to the days of his youthful vigor." (Job 33:25) The day will come when no one will have reason to say, "I am sick." Why? Because God-fearing humans will be relieved of the burden of sin and its grievous effects. (Isaiah 33:24; Luke 13:11-13) Yes, God "will wipe out every tear from their eyes, and death will be no more, neither will mourning nor outcry nor pain be anymore. The former things have passed away."—Revelation 21:4.

14 Attaining perfection, however, involves much more than having a sound body and a sound mind. It includes properly reflecting Jehovah's qualities, since we were made 'in God's image, according to his likeness.' (Genesis 1:26) To that end, much education will be required. In the new world, "righteousness is to dwell." So, as Isaiah foretold, "righteousness is what

---

13. What physical benefits will be realized under Kingdom rule?
14. What does attaining human perfection include?

the inhabitants of the productive land will certainly learn." (2 Peter 3:13; Isaiah 26:9) This quality leads to peace—between people of all races, among close associates, in one's family and, above all, with God himself. (Psalm 85:10-13; Isaiah 32:17) Those who learn righteousness will progressively be educated in God's will for them. As love for Jehovah becomes deeply rooted in their hearts, they will follow his ways in every aspect of their lives. They will be able to say as did Jesus, 'I always do the things pleasing to my Father.' (John 8:29) How enjoyable life will be when that is true of all humankind!

Accomplishments Already Evident

15 The impressive accomplishments of God's Kingdom and its subjects are evident. The following questions and scriptures will remind you of some of these accomplishments, as well as of things that all subjects of the Kingdom can and should be doing now.

Against whom did the Kingdom first take action, and with what result? (Revelation 12:7-10, 12)

The gathering of the remaining members of what group is being given attention since Christ was enthroned? (Revelation 14:1-3)

What work did Jesus foretell that he would do after the outbreak of the great tribulation, as recorded at Matthew 25:31-33?

What preliminary work is being accomplished to-

---

15. Using the questions in this paragraph, highlight accomplishments of the Kingdom and show what we should be doing now.

day? Who are participating in it? (Psalm 110:3; Matthew 24:14; Revelation 14:6, 7)

Why have political and religious opposers been unable to stop the preaching work? (Zechariah 4:6; Acts 5:38, 39)

What changes have taken place in the lives of those who submit to Kingdom rule? (Isaiah 2:4; 1 Corinthians 6:9-11)

Kingdom of a Thousand Years

16 After the abyssing of Satan and his demons, Jesus Christ and his 144,000 joint heirs will rule as kings and priests for the thousand years. (Revelation 20:6) During that period, mankind will be brought to perfection, with sin and Adamic death forever eliminated. At the end of the Thousand Year Reign, having successfully carried out his assignment as Messianic King-Priest, Jesus "hands over the kingdom" to his Father, "that God may be all things to everyone." (1 Corinthians 15:24-28) At that point, Satan is released for a little while to test redeemed humankind as to their support of Jehovah's universal sovereignty. After that final test is complete, Jehovah will destroy Satan and the rebels who sided with him. (Revelation 20:7-10) Those who upheld Jehovah's sovereignty–his right to rule–will have fully demonstrated their unswerving loyalty. They will then be brought into their proper relationship with Jehovah, being accepted by him as his sons and daughters, divinely approved for everlasting life.–Romans 8:21.

---

16. (a) How long will Christ rule? (b) What marvelous things will be done during and after that time?

[17] Therefore, Jesus' own function and that of the 144,000 will change in relation to the earth. What will their future activity be? The Bible does not say. But if we faithfully uphold Jehovah's sovereignty, we will be alive at the end of the Thousand Year Reign to find out what Jehovah has purposed for them as well as for his awesome universe. Nevertheless, Christ's thousand-year rulership will be "indefinitely lasting" and his Kingdom "will not be brought to ruin." (Daniel 7:14) In what sense? For one thing, the ruling authority will not pass into the hands of others who have different aims, as Jehovah will be Ruler. Also, the Kingdom "will never be brought to ruin" because its accomplishments will endure forever. (Daniel 2:44) And the Messianic King-Priest and his associate king-priests will forever be honored because of their faithful service to Jehovah.

---

17. (a) What will happen to the Kingdom at the end of the thousand years? (b) In what sense is it true that the Kingdom "will never be brought to ruin"?

Review Discussion

- Why is God's Kingdom the only solution to mankind's problems? When did the King of God's Kingdom begin to rule?
- What is especially appealing to you about God's Kingdom and what it will accomplish?
- What accomplishments of the Kingdom can we already see, and what part do we have in these?

CHAPTER ELEVEN

'Keep On Seeking First the Kingdom'

OVER 1,900 years ago in a discourse in Galilee, Jesus urged his hearers: "Keep on, then, seeking first the kingdom and [God's] righteousness." But why such urgency? Was not the time for Christ to receive Kingdom power many centuries off? Yes, but the Messianic Kingdom was to be the means by which Jehovah would vindicate his sovereignty and fulfill his grand purpose for the earth. Anyone who truly appreciated the importance of those things would give the Kingdom first place in his life. If that was true in the first century, how much more so it is today, now that Christ has been enthroned as King! So the question is, Does my way of life show that I am seeking God's Kingdom first?—Matthew 6:33.

2 Today, millions of people throughout the world are, in fact, seeking first the Kingdom. They are showing their support of Kingdom rule by centering their lives on the doing of Jehovah's will, having dedicated themselves to him. On the other hand, the vast majority of humankind is interested in seeking mundane things. People pursue money and the possessions and pleasures that money can buy. Or they put their main

---

1. (a) Why did Jesus urge his hearers to seek first the Kingdom? (b) What question should we ask ourselves?
2. What things do people in general eagerly pursue?

energies into furthering their careers. Their way of life reflects a preoccupation with themselves, material things, and pleasures. They put God in second place, if they believe in him at all.—Matthew 6:31, 32.

3 To his disciples, however, Jesus gave this counsel: "Stop storing up for yourselves treasures upon the earth," since none of such possessions last forever. "Rather," he said, "store up for yourselves treasures in heaven" by serving Jehovah. Jesus urged his followers to keep their eye "simple" by focusing attention and energies on the doing of God's will. "You cannot slave for God and for Riches," he told them. But what about material needs—food, clothing, and shelter? "Stop being anxious," Jesus counseled. He directed their attention to the birds—God feeds them. Jesus encouraged his followers to take a lesson from the flowers—God clothes them. Are not Jehovah's intelligent human servants worth more than any of these? "Keep on, then, seeking first the kingdom and his righteousness," Jesus said, "and all these other [necessary] things will be added to you." (Matthew 6:19-34) Do your actions show that you believe that?

Do Not Let Kingdom Truth Be Choked Out

4 It is proper to be concerned about having enough to meet the material needs of oneself and one's family. If a person is excessively concerned about material things, however, the results can be disastrous. Even

---

3. (a) What kind of treasures did Jesus encourage his disciples to seek, and why? (b) Why is there no need to be overly concerned about material things?
4. If a person puts too much emphasis on material things, what may be the outcome?

though he may profess to believe in the Kingdom, if in his heart he puts other things first, Kingdom truth will be choked out. (Matthew 13:18-22) For example, on one occasion a rich young ruler asked Jesus: "What must I do to inherit everlasting life?" He led a moral life and treated others well, but he was overly attached to his material possessions. He could not bring himself to part with them in order to become a follower of Christ. So he passed up an opportunity that could have led to his being with Christ in the heavenly Kingdom. Jesus said on that occasion: "How difficult a thing it will be for those with money to enter into the kingdom of God!"—Mark 10:17-23.

5 Years later, the apostle Paul wrote to Timothy, who was then in Ephesus, a prosperous commercial center. Paul reminded him: "We have brought nothing into the world, and neither can we carry anything out. So, having sustenance and covering, we shall be content with these things." Working to provide "sustenance and covering" for oneself and one's family is proper. But Paul warned: "Those who are determined to be rich fall into temptation and a snare and many senseless and hurtful desires, which plunge men into destruction and ruin." Satan is subtle. At first he may entice a person in small ways. This may be followed by greater pressure, perhaps an opportunity for a promotion or a better job that pays more but demands time formerly set aside for spiritual matters. Unless we are on guard, "the love of money" can choke out the far

---

5. (a) With what things did Paul encourage Timothy to be content, and why? (b) How does Satan use "the love of money" as a destructive snare?

more important Kingdom interests. Paul put it this way: "By reaching out for this love some have been led astray from the faith and have stabbed themselves all over with many pains."—1 Timothy 6:7-10.

6 With genuine love for his Christian brother, Paul urged Timothy: "Flee from these things" and, "Fight the fine fight of the faith." (1 Timothy 6:11, 12) Earnest effort is needed if we are to avoid being swept along by the materialistic way of life of the world around us. But if we exert ourselves in harmony with our faith, Jehovah will never forsake us. Regardless of high prices and widespread unemployment, he will make sure that we have what we really need. Paul wrote: "Let your manner of life be free of the love of money, while you are content with the present things. For [God] has said: 'I will by no means leave you nor by any means forsake you.' So that we may be of good courage and say: 'Jehovah is my helper; I will not be afraid. What can man do to me?'" (Hebrews 13:5, 6) And King David wrote: "A young man I used to be, I have also grown old, and yet I have not seen anyone righteous left entirely, nor his offspring looking for bread."—Psalm 37:25.

Early Disciples Provide a Pattern

7 After Jesus gave his apostles suitable training, he sent them out in Israel to preach the good news and

---

6. (a) To avoid being ensnared by materialism, what must we do? (b) What confidence can we have even in view of the world's economic situation today?

7. What instructions regarding preaching did Jesus give his disciples, and why were these appropriate?

declare: "The kingdom of the heavens has drawn near." What a thrilling message it was! Jesus Christ, the Messianic King, was in their midst. Since the apostles were devoting themselves to the service of God, Jesus urged them to have confidence that God would care for them. So he said: "Carry nothing for the trip, neither staff nor food pouch, nor bread nor silver money; neither have two undergarments. But wherever you enter into a home, stay there and leave from there." (Matthew 10:5-10; Luke 9:1-6) Jehovah would see to it that their needs were satisfied at the hands of fellow Israelites, among whom hospitality to strangers was customary.

8 Later, just before his death, Jesus alerted his apostles to the fact that in the future they would be working under changed circumstances. As a result of official opposition to their activity, hospitality might not be so readily extended to them in Israel. Also, they would soon be carrying the Kingdom message to Gentile lands. Now they *were* to take along "a purse" and "a food pouch." Nevertheless, they were to keep on seeking first Jehovah's Kingdom and his righteousness, confident that God would bless their efforts to obtain needed sustenance and covering.—Luke 22:35-37.

9 The apostle Paul was a fine example of one who

---

8. (a) Shortly before his death, why did Jesus give new preaching instructions? (b) What was still to be first in the lives of Jesus' followers?
9. How did Paul put the Kingdom first in his life while caring for his physical needs, and what counsel did he give on this matter?

applied Jesus' counsel. Paul built his life around the ministry. (Acts 20:24, 25) When he went into an area to preach, he took care of his own material needs, even working at tentmaking. He did not expect others to look after him. (Acts 18:1-4; 1 Thessalonians 2:9) Yet, he gratefully accepted hospitality and gifts when others expressed their love in this way. (Acts 16:15, 34; Philippians 4:15-17) Paul encouraged Christians, not to neglect their family obligations in order to preach, but rather to balance their varied responsibilities. He counseled them to work, to love their families, and to share with others. (Ephesians 4:28; 2 Thessalonians 3: 7-12) He urged them to put confidence in God, not in material possessions, and to use their lives in a way that showed that they really understood what the more important things are. In harmony with Jesus' teachings, that meant seeking first God's Kingdom and his righteousness.—Philippians 1:9-11.

Keep the Kingdom First in Your Life

10 To what extent do we personally share the Kingdom good news with others? That depends, in part, on our circumstances and on the depth of our appreciation. Keep in mind that Jesus did not say, 'Seek the Kingdom when you have nothing else to do.' Knowing the importance of the Kingdom, he expressed his Father's will, saying: "Seek continually his kingdom." (Luke 12:31) Although most of us need to work to care for the needs of ourselves and our families, if we have faith, our lives will revolve around the Kingdom

---

10. What does it mean to seek first the Kingdom?

work that God has given us. At the same time, we will care for our family responsibilities.—1 Timothy 5:8.

11 Some of us are able to devote more time than others to preaching the good news of the Kingdom. But in his parable concerning various kinds of soil, Jesus showed that all whose hearts are like fine soil will bear fruit. To what extent? The circumstances of individuals vary. Age, health, and family responsibilities are all factors. But when there is genuine appreciation, much can be accomplished.—Matthew 13:23.

12 It is good to have goals that will help us to expand our share in the Kingdom ministry. Young ones should think seriously about the excellent example of that zealous young Christian Timothy. (Philippians 2:19-22) What could be finer than for them to enter the full-time ministry when

---

11. (a) How did Jesus illustrate that not all would be able to do the same amount in spreading the Kingdom message? (b) What factors have a bearing on how much one can do?
12. What wholesome spiritual goal are young ones especially encouraged to consider?

In every land, Jehovah's Witnesses today are preaching the good news, before the end comes

they complete their secular schooling? Older ones too will benefit by setting wholesome spiritual goals.

13 Rather than criticizing those who we might feel could do more, we should be moved by faith to work for personal improvement so that we might serve God to the full extent that *our own* circumstances permit. (Romans 14:10-12; Galatians 6:4, 5) As shown in the case of Job, Satan contends that our main interests are our material possessions, our own comfort, and our personal well-being and that our motive in serving God is a selfish one. But if we are truly seeking first the Kingdom, we are having a share in proving the Devil to be the gross liar that he is. We are giving evidence that what comes first in our lives is the service of God. In word and deed, we thus prove our deep love for Jehovah, our loyal support of his sovereignty, and our love for fellowmen.—Job 1:9-11; 2:4, 5; Proverbs 27:11.

14 A schedule can help us to accomplish more than we might otherwise get done. Jehovah himself has "an appointed time" for carrying out his purpose. (Exodus 9:5; Mark 1:15) If possible, it is good to share in the field ministry at one or more appointed times each week. Hundreds of thousands of Jehovah's Witnesses around the world have enrolled as auxiliary pioneers, spending about two hours a day in preaching the good news. Hundreds of thousands of others serve

---

13. (a) Who decides what we are personally able to do in Kingdom service? (b) If we truly seek first the Kingdom, what do we prove?

14. (a) Why is a schedule for the field ministry beneficial? (b) To what extent are many Witnesses sharing in the field ministry?

as regular pioneers, using some two and a half hours a day to proclaim the Kingdom message. Special pioneers and missionaries spend even more time in Kingdom service. We can also seek opportunities to share the Kingdom hope informally with any who will listen. (John 4:7-15) Our desire should be to have as full a share in that work as our circumstances permit, for Jesus foretold: "This good news of the kingdom will be preached in all the inhabited earth for a witness to all the nations; and then the end will come."—Matthew 24:14; Ephesians 5:15-17.

15 Unitedly, in all parts of the earth, regardless of the nation in which they live, Jehovah's Witnesses are sharing in this privilege of service. They apply to themselves the inspired Bible counsel: "Become steadfast, unmovable, always having plenty to do in the work of the Lord, knowing that your labor is not in vain in connection with the Lord."—1 Corinthians 15:58.

---

15. In connection with our ministry, why do you feel that the counsel at 1 Corinthians 15:58 is timely?

Review Discussion

- When Jesus said to keep on "seeking first the kingdom," what was he indicating should be put in a secondary place?
- What should be our viewpoint toward caring for the physical needs of ourselves and our families? What help will God give us?
- In what features of Kingdom service can we share?

CHAPTER TWELVE

The Meaning of Your Baptism

IN THE year 29 C.E., Jesus was baptized, being immersed by John the Baptizer in the Jordan River. Jehovah himself was watching and expressed approval. (Matthew 3:16, 17) Jesus thus set a pattern that all of his disciples would follow. Three and a half years later, Jesus gave these instructions to his disciples: "All authority has been given me in heaven and on the earth. Go therefore and make disciples of people of all the nations, baptizing them in the name of the Father and of the Son and of the holy spirit." (Matthew 28: 18, 19) Have you been baptized in harmony with what Jesus there directed? If not, are you preparing to do so?

2 In either case, a clear understanding of baptism is important for everyone who wants to serve Jehovah and live in his righteous new world. Questions that deserve answers include these: Does Christian baptism today have the same meaning as that of Jesus' baptism? What does it mean to be baptized "in the name of the Father and of the Son and of the holy spirit"? What is involved in living in accord with what Christian water baptism signifies?

---

1. Why should water baptism be of personal interest to each of us?

2. In connection with baptism, what questions need to be answered?

Baptisms Performed by John

3 About six months before Jesus was baptized, John the Baptizer went preaching in the wilderness of Judea, saying: "Repent, for the kingdom of the heavens has drawn near." (Matthew 3:1, 2) People heard what John said and took it to heart. They openly confessed their sins, repented of them, and then came to John to be baptized by him in the Jordan River. That baptism was for the Jews.—Luke 1:13-16; Acts 13:23, 24.

4 Those Jews were urgently in need of repentance. At Mount Sinai in the year 1513 B.C.E., their forefathers had entered into a national covenant—a formal, solemn agreement—with Jehovah God. But because of their gross sins, they did not live up to their responsibilities under that covenant, so they were condemned by it. By Jesus' day their situation was critical. "The great and fear-inspiring day of Jehovah" foretold by Malachi was near. In 70 C.E., that "day" came when Roman armies destroyed Jerusalem, its temple, and over a million Jews. John the Baptizer, with a zeal for true worship, was sent in advance of that destruction, "to get ready for Jehovah a prepared people." They needed to repent of their sins against the Mosaic Law covenant and be prepared to accept the Son of God, Jesus, whom Jehovah was sending to them.—Malachi 4:4-6; Luke 1:17; Acts 19:4.

5 Among those who came to John to be baptized was

---

3. To whom was John's baptism limited?
4. Why did the Jews in the first century urgently need to repent?
5. (a) When Jesus came to be baptized, why did John question this? (b) What was symbolized by Jesus' baptism?

Jesus himself. But why? Knowing that Jesus had no sins to confess, John said: "I am the one needing to be baptized by you, and are you coming to me?" But Jesus' baptism was to symbolize something different. So Jesus replied: "Let it be, this time, for in that way it is suitable for us to carry out all that is righteous." (Matthew 3:13-15) Because Jesus was without sin, his baptism did not symbolize repentance over sin; nor did he need to dedicate himself to God, since he was a member of a nation already dedicated to Jehovah. Rather, his baptism at 30 years of age was unique to him, and it symbolized *the presenting of himself to his heavenly Father to do His further will.*

6 God's will for Christ Jesus involved activity in connection with the Kingdom. (Luke 8:1) It also involved the sacrifice of his perfect human life as a ransom and as the basis for a new covenant. (Matthew 20:28; 26:26-28; Hebrews 10:5-10) Jesus took very seriously what his water baptism symbolized. He did not allow his attention to be diverted to other interests. To the end of his earthly life, he stuck to the doing of God's will, making the preaching of God's Kingdom his main work.—John 4:34.

Water Baptism of Christian Disciples

7 Jesus' first disciples were baptized in water by John and then directed to Jesus as prospective members of the Kingdom of heaven. (John 3:25-30) Under Jesus' direction these disciples also did some baptizing,

---

6. How serious was Jesus about doing God's will for him?
7. Since Pentecost 33 C.E., what were Christians told to do in connection with baptism?

which had the same significance as John's baptism. (John 4:1, 2) However, starting with Pentecost 33 C.E., they began to fulfill the commission to baptize "in the name of the Father and of the Son and of the holy spirit." (Matthew 28:19) You will find it very beneficial to review what that means.

8 What does it mean to be baptized "in the name of the Father"? It means accepting his name, office, authority, purpose, and laws. Consider what this involves. (1) Concerning his name, Psalm 83:18 says: "You, whose name is Jehovah, you alone are the Most High over all the earth." (2) Regarding his office, 2 Kings 19:15 states: "O Jehovah . . . , you alone are the true God." (3) Of his authority, Revelation 4:11 tells us: "You are worthy, Jehovah, even our God, to receive the glory and the honor and the power, because you created all things, and because of your will they existed and were created." (4) We must also acknowledge that Jehovah is the Life-Giver, who purposes to save us from sin and death: "Salvation belongs to Jehovah." (Psalm 3:8; 36:9) (5) We need to accept that Jehovah is the Supreme Law-Giver: "Jehovah is our Judge, Jehovah is our Statute-giver, Jehovah is our King." (Isaiah 33:22) Because he is all those things, we are urged: "You must love Jehovah your God with your whole heart and with your whole soul and with your whole mind."—Matthew 22:37.

9 What does baptism "in the name . . . of the Son"

---

8. What does it mean to be baptized "in the name of the Father"?
9. What does it mean to be baptized "in the name . . . of the Son"?

mean? It means recognizing the name, office, and authority of Jesus Christ. His name, Jesus, means "Jehovah Is Salvation." He derives his office from the fact that he is God's only-begotten Son, the first of God's creation. (Matthew 16:16; Colossians 1:15, 16) Of this Son, John 3:16 tells us: "God loved the world [of redeemable mankind] so much that he gave his only-begotten Son, in order that everyone exercising faith in him might not be destroyed but have everlasting life." Because Jesus died faithful, God resurrected him from the dead and gave him new authority. According to the apostle Paul, God "exalted [Jesus] to a superior position" in the universe, second only to Jehovah. That is why "in the name of Jesus every knee should bend . . . and every tongue should openly acknowledge that Jesus Christ is Lord to the glory of God the Father." (Philippians 2:9-11) This means obeying Jesus' commandments, which issue from Jehovah himself. —John 15:10.

10 What does it mean to be baptized "in the name . . . of the holy spirit"? It means acknowledging the function and activity of the holy spirit. And what is the holy spirit? It is Jehovah's active force, with which he accomplishes his purposes. Jesus told his followers: "I will request the Father and he will give you another helper to be with you forever, the spirit of the truth." (John 14:16, 17) What would this enable them to do? Jesus further told them: "You will receive power when the holy spirit arrives upon you, and you will be witnesses of me both in Jerusalem and in all Judea and

---

10. What does it mean to be baptized "in the name . . . of the holy spirit"?

Samaria and to the most distant part of the earth." (Acts 1:8) By means of the holy spirit, Jehovah also inspired the writing of the Bible: "Prophecy was at no time brought by man's will, but men spoke from God as they were borne along by holy spirit." (2 Peter 1:21) So we acknowledge the role of the holy spirit when we study the Bible. Another way we acknowledge the holy spirit is by asking Jehovah to help us produce "the fruitage of the spirit," which is "love, joy, peace, long-suffering, kindness, goodness, faith, mildness, self-control."—Galatians 5:22, 23.

11 The first ones to be baptized in harmony with Jesus' instructions were Jews and Jewish proselytes, beginning in 33 C.E. Shortly thereafter, the privilege of Christian discipleship was extended to the Samaritans. Then, in 36 C.E., the call widened out to include uncircumcised Gentiles. Before being baptized, the Samaritans and Gentiles had to make *a personal dedication to Jehovah to serve him as disciples of his Son.* This continues to be the significance of Christian water baptism down to our day. Complete immersion in water is a fitting symbol of this personal dedication, as baptism is a symbolic burial. Your going beneath the baptismal waters represents your dying to your former life course. Being raised out of the water symbolizes your being made alive to do God's will. This "one baptism" applies to all who become true Christians. At baptism they become Christian Witnesses of Jehovah, God's ordained ministers.—Ephesians 4:5; 2 Corinthians 6:3, 4.

---

11. (a) What is the true significance of baptism in our day? (b) How is baptism like dying and being raised up?

12 Such baptism has great saving value in the eyes of God. For instance, after mentioning Noah's constructing of the ark, in which he and his family were preserved through the Flood, the apostle Peter wrote: "That which corresponds to this is also *now saving you,* namely, baptism, (not the putting away of the filth of the flesh, but the request made to God for a good conscience,) through the resurrection of Jesus Christ." (1 Peter 3:21) The ark was tangible evidence that Noah had faithfully done the work assigned by God. After work on the ark was finished, "the world of that time suffered destruction when it was deluged with water." (2 Peter 3:6) But Noah and his family, "eight souls, were carried safely through the water."—1 Peter 3:20.

13 Today, those who dedicate themselves to Jehovah on the basis of faith in the resurrected Christ get baptized in symbol of that dedication. They proceed to do God's will for our day and are saved from the present

---

12. To what does Christian water baptism correspond, and how?
13. From what is a Christian saved through water baptism?

To relatives

To workmates

To schoolmates

On the streets

By returning to visit interested ones

At home Bible studies

SOME WAYS TO PROCLAIM THE KINGDOM

From door to door

wicked world. (Galatians 1:3, 4) No longer are they headed for destruction with the present wicked system of things. They are saved from this and are granted a good conscience by God. The apostle John assures God's servants: "The world is passing away and so is its desire, but he that does the will of God remains forever."—1 John 2:17.

Living Up to Our Responsibilities

14 It would be a mistake to conclude that baptism is in itself a guarantee of salvation. It has value only if a person has truly dedicated himself to Jehovah through Jesus Christ and thereafter carries out God's will, being faithful to the end. "He that has endured to the end is the one that will be saved."—Matthew 24:13.

15 God's will for Jesus included how he used his life as a human. It was to be laid down in death as a sacrifice. In our case, our bodies are to be presented to God, and we are to carry on a self-sacrificing life by doing God's will. (Romans 12:1, 2) We would certainly not be doing God's will if even occasionally we deliberately conducted ourselves like the world around us or if we built our lives around selfish pursuits, giving only token service to God. (1 Peter 4:1-3; 1 John 2:15, 16) When a certain Jew asked what he must do to get everlasting life, Jesus acknowledged the importance of living a morally clean life. But then he pointed to something even more important: the need to be a Christian disciple, a follower of Jesus. That must be

---

14. Why is baptism in itself not a guarantee of salvation?
15. (a) What is God's will today for baptized Christians? (b) How important should Christian discipleship be in our lives?

the main thing in life. It cannot take second place to material pursuits.—Matthew 19:16-21.

16 It should again be emphasized that God's will for Jesus included vital activity in connection with God's Kingdom. Jesus was himself anointed to be King. But while on earth, he also gave a zealous witness concerning the Kingdom. We have a similar witnessing work to do, and we have every reason to engage in it wholeheartedly. By so doing, we demonstrate our appreciation for Jehovah's sovereignty as well as our love for fellow humans. (Matthew 22:36-40) We also show that we are united with fellow worshipers worldwide, all of whom are Kingdom proclaimers. Together, in global unity, we press on toward the goal of everlasting life in the earthly realm of that Kingdom.

---

16. (a) What responsibility do all Christians have in connection with the Kingdom? (b) As illustrated on pages 116 and 117, what are some effective ways in which to do the Kingdom work? (c) Our wholehearted share in the witnessing work gives evidence of what?

Review Discussion

- What similarities and what differences are there between Jesus' baptism and water baptism today?
- What does it mean to be baptized "in the name of the Father and of the Son and of the holy spirit"?
- What is involved in living up to the responsibilities of Christian water baptism?

CHAPTER THIRTEEN

A Great Crowd Before Jehovah's Throne

FAITHFUL servants of God from Abel to John the Baptizer put the doing of God's will first in their lives. Yet, they all died, waiting for their resurrection to life on earth in God's new world. The 144,000, who will rule with Christ in God's heavenly Kingdom, must also die before they can receive their reward. However, Revelation 7:9 shows that in these last days, there would be "a great crowd" out of all nations who would not experience death but would have the prospect of living forever on earth. Are you among them?

Identifying the Great Crowd

2 In 1923, Jehovah's servants discerned that "the sheep" of Jesus' parable found at Matthew 25:31-46 and the "other sheep" to which he referred as recorded at John 10:16 are people who would have the opportunity to live forever on earth. In 1931 those described at Ezekiel 9:1-11 as being marked in their foreheads were also seen to be those with the earthly hope. Then in 1935 it was learned that the great crowd form part of

---

1. (a) Before either pre-Christian servants of God or the 144,000 receive their reward, what must they experience? (b) What will be possible for "a great crowd" who are living at this time?
2. What led up to a clear understanding of the identity of the great crowd of Revelation 7:9?

the other sheep class Jesus spoke about. Today, this favored great crowd numbers in the millions.

3 At Revelation 7:9, the great crowd is not seen as being in heaven. Their "standing before the throne" of God does not require them to be in heaven. They are simply in the sight of God. (Psalm 11:4) The fact that the great crowd, "which no man was able to number," is not a heavenly class is shown by comparing its unspecified number with what is written at Revelation 7:4-8 and Revelation 14:1-4. There the number taken from the earth to heaven is revealed to be 144,000.

4 Revelation 7:14 says of the great crowd: "These are the ones that come out of the great tribulation." They survive the worst trouble ever experienced in human history. (Matthew 24:21) When they thankfully attribute their salvation to God and to Christ, then all faithful creatures in heaven will unite with them in saying: "Amen! The blessing and the glory and the wisdom and the thanksgiving and the honor and the power and the strength be to our God forever and ever. Amen."—Revelation 7:11, 12.

Proving Worthy

5 The preservation of the great crowd through the great tribulation takes place in harmony with Jehovah's righteous standards. The identifying traits

---

3. Why does the expression "standing before the throne" not refer to a heavenly class?

4. (a) What is "the great tribulation" that the great crowd survive? (b) As stated at Revelation 7:11, 12, who observe the great crowd and share with them in worship?

5. How can we determine what is required to be part of the great crowd?

of those who will be delivered are clearly discussed in the Bible. Thus, it is possible for lovers of righteousness to act now with a view to proving worthy of survival. What must these ones do?

6 Sheep are mild-tempered and submissive. So when Jesus said that he had other sheep who were not of the heavenly class, he meant people who not only would want to live forever on earth but also would be submissive to his teachings. "My sheep listen to my voice, and I know them, and they follow me," he said. (John 10:16, 27) These are people who really listen to and obediently do what Jesus says, becoming his disciples.

7 What other qualities would each of these followers of Jesus need to develop? God's Word answers: "You should put away the old personality which conforms to your former course of conduct and . . . should put on the new personality which was created according to God's will in true righteousness and loyalty." (Ephesians 4:22-24) They develop qualities that enhance the unity of God's servants—"love, joy, peace, long-suffering, kindness, goodness, faith, mildness, self-control."—Galatians 5:22, 23.

8 The great crowd support the small number of those with heavenly hopes, who take the lead in the preaching work. (Matthew 24:14; 25:40) The other sheep give this support, although they know that they will face opposition because at the beginning of these last days, Christ Jesus and his angels cast Satan

---

6. Why can the great crowd properly be likened to sheep?
7. What qualities do the followers of Jesus need to develop?
8. What will the great crowd face as they support the remnant?

and his demons out of heaven. This meant "woe for the earth . . . because the Devil has come down to you, having great anger, knowing he has a short period of time." (Revelation 12:7-12) Thus, Satan intensifies opposition to God's servants as this system's end draws near.

9 In spite of vicious persecution, the preaching work continues to advance. From only a few thousand Kingdom preachers at the end of World War I, there

9. How successful are God's servants in preaching the good news, and why?

Millions of the great crowd unitedly worship the true God

are now millions, for Jehovah promised: "Any weapon whatever that will be formed against you will have no success." (Isaiah 54:17) Even a member of the Jewish high court recognized that a work of God could not be defeated. He told the Pharisees in the first century regarding the disciples: "Let them alone; (because, if this scheme or this work is from men, it will be overthrown; but if it is from God, you will not be able to overthrow them;) otherwise, you may perhaps be found fighters actually against God."—Acts 5: 38, 39.

10 Those of the great crowd are pictured as being marked for survival. (Ezekiel 9:4-6) "The mark" is the evidence that they are dedicated to Jehovah, baptized as disciples of Jesus, and involved in cultivating a Christlike personality. They obey the "voice out of heaven" that says regarding Satan's worldwide empire of false religion: "Get out of her, my people, if you do not want to share with her in her sins, and if you do not want to receive part of her plagues."—Revelation 18:1-5.

11 Also, Jesus told his followers: "By this all will know that you are my disciples, if you have love among yourselves." (John 13:35) In contrast, members of this world's religions kill other members in war, often just because they are of different nationalities! God's Word states: "The children of God and the children of the

---

10. (a) What does "the mark" on those of the great crowd mean? (b) How do God's servants obey the "voice out of heaven"?
11. In what important way do those of the great crowd demonstrate that they are Jehovah's servants?

Devil are evident by this fact: Everyone who does not carry on righteousness does not originate with God, neither does he who does not love his brother. . . . We should have love for one another; not like Cain, who originated with the wicked one and slaughtered his brother."—1 John 3:10-12.

12 Jesus declared: "Every good tree produces fine fruit, but every rotten tree produces worthless fruit; a good tree cannot bear worthless fruit, neither can a rotten tree produce fine fruit. Every tree not producing fine fruit gets cut down and thrown into the fire. Really, then, by their fruits you will recognize those men." (Matthew 7:17-20) The fruitage produced by this world's religions identifies them as rotten 'trees,' soon to be destroyed by Jehovah at the great tribulation.—Revelation 17:16.

13 Revelation 7:9-15 draws attention to factors that lead to the preservation of the great crowd. They are shown unitedly "standing before the throne" of Jehovah, upholding his universal sovereignty. They have "washed their robes and made them white in the blood of the Lamb," showing that they recognize the sin-atoning sacrifice of Jesus. (John 1:29) They have dedicated themselves to God and have symbolized this by water immersion. So they enjoy a clean standing before God, pictured by the white robes, and render him "sacred service day and night." Are there

---

12. At the great tribulation, how will Jehovah deal with religious 'trees' that produce worthless fruitage?
13. How do the great crowd demonstrate that they are unitedly "standing before the throne" of Jehovah?

ways you can bring your life more fully into line with what is here described?

Benefits Now

14 Likely you have observed the unique benefits that even now come to those serving Jehovah. As an example, when you learned about Jehovah's righteous purposes, you understood that there was a bright hope for the future. So now you have a real purpose in life —to serve the true God with the joyful prospect of eternal life on a paradise earth. Yes, the King Jesus Christ "will guide [the great crowd] to fountains of waters of life."—Revelation 7:17.

15 A marvelous benefit enjoyed by the great crowd is the love, unity, and harmony found among Jehovah's servants earth wide. Since we all feed on the same spiritual food, we all obey the same laws and principles found in God's Word. That is why we are not divided by political or national ideologies. Too, we maintain the high moral standards that God requires of his people. (1 Corinthians 6:9-11) Thus, rather than experiencing the strife, disunity, and immorality prevalent in the world, Jehovah's people enjoy what can be called a spiritual paradise. Note how this is described at Isaiah 65:13, 14.

16 No, Jehovah's human servants are not perfect. And

---

14. What are some of the unique benefits that come to Jehovah's servants even now?
15. How are Jehovah's Witnesses benefited by holding to Bible principles regarding political and moral matters?
16. Despite problems common to life, those of the great crowd have what hope?

they are affected by problems common to life in this world, such as falling on hard times or becoming innocent victims in the wars of the nations. They also face sickness, suffering, and death. But they have faith that in the new world, God "will wipe out every tear from their eyes, and death will be no more, neither will mourning nor outcry nor pain be anymore."—Revelation 21:4.

17 Even if you lose your life now because of old age, sickness, an accident, or persecution, Jehovah will resurrect you to life in Paradise. (Acts 24:15) Then you will continue to enjoy a spiritual feast during the Millennial Reign of Christ. Your love of God will deepen as you see his purposes come to glorious realization. And the physical blessings that Jehovah will then provide will further deepen your love for him. (Isaiah 25:6-9) What a marvelous future is in store for God's people!

---

17. Regardless of what may happen to us now, what marvelous future is in store for those who worship the true God?

Review Discussion

- With what extraordinary event does the Bible associate the great crowd?
- If we really want to be included in that divinely favored great crowd, what must we do now?
- How important to you are the blessings that the great crowd now enjoys and will yet enjoy in God's new world?

CHAPTER FOURTEEN

How Does Jehovah Direct His Organization?

DOES God have an organization? The inspired Scriptures tell us that he does. In his Word, he gives us glimpses of the awesome heavenly part of that organization. (Ezekiel 1:1, 4-14; Daniel 7:9, 10, 13, 14) Although we cannot see this invisible part, it greatly affects true worshipers today. (2 Kings 6:15-17) Jehovah's organization also has a visible part, on earth. The Bible helps us to understand what it is and how Jehovah directs it.

Identifying the Visible Part

2 For 1,545 years the nation of Israel was the congregation of God. (Acts 7:38) But Israel failed to keep God's laws and rejected his own Son. As a result, Jehovah rejected that congregation and cast it off. Jesus told the Jews: "Look! Your house is abandoned to you." (Matthew 23:38) God then brought into existence a new congregation, with which he made a new covenant. This congregation was to be made up of 144,000 individuals chosen by God to be united with his Son in heaven.—Revelation 14:1-4.

---

1. What information about Jehovah's organization does the Bible reveal, and why is it important to us?
2. What new congregation did God bring into existence?

3 The first ones of that new congregation were anointed with Jehovah's holy spirit at Pentecost 33 C.E. Concerning that remarkable event, we read: "Now while the day of the festival of Pentecost was in progress they were all together at the same place, and suddenly there occurred from heaven a noise just like that of a rushing stiff breeze, and it filled the whole house in which they were sitting. And tongues as if of fire became visible to them and were distributed about, and one sat upon each one of them, and they all became filled with holy spirit." (Acts 2: 1-4) Thus God's spirit gave clear evidence that this was now the body of people that God would use to accomplish his purpose under the direction of Jesus Christ in heaven.

4 Today, only a remnant of the 144,000 are on earth. But in fulfillment of Bible prophecy, "a great crowd" of "other sheep," millions of them, have been brought into association with the anointed remnant. Jesus, the Fine Shepherd, has merged these other sheep with the remnant so that they form just one flock under him as their one Shepherd. (Revelation 7:9; John 10:11, 16) These all make up one united congregation, Jehovah's visible organization.

Theocratic in Structure

5 The Scriptural expression "the congregation of the living God" makes evident who directs it. The organization is theocratic, or God-ruled. Jehovah provides

---

3. What took place at Pentecost 33 C.E. as clear evidence that God was now using a new congregation?
4. Who today make up Jehovah's visible organization?
5. Who directs God's organization, and how?

direction for his people through Jesus, the one He appointed to be the invisible Head of the congregation, and by means of His own inspired Word, the Bible. —1 Timothy 3:14, 15; Ephesians 1:22, 23; 2 Timothy 3: 16, 17.

6 Such direction was very evident at Pentecost. (Acts 2:14-18, 32, 33) It was manifest when Jehovah's angel directed the spreading of the good news into Africa, when Jesus' voice gave directions at the conversion of Saul of Tarsus, and when Peter began the preaching work among the Gentiles. (Acts 8:26, 27; 9:3-7; 10: 9-16, 19-22) But, in time, no more voices were heard from heaven, no more angels were seen, no more miraculous gifts of the spirit were bestowed. Yet, Jesus had promised: "Look! I am with you all the days until the conclusion of the system of things." (Matthew 28: 20; 1 Corinthians 13:8) Today, Jehovah's Witnesses acknowledge Jesus' direction. Without that, proclaiming the Kingdom message in the face of intense hostility would be impossible.

7 Shortly before his death, Jesus told his disciples about "the faithful and discreet slave" that he as Master would entrust with special responsibility. That "slave" would be on hand when the Lord departed for heaven and would still be working hard at Christ's invisible return in Kingdom power. Such a description could hardly fit one individual, but it does fit Christ's

6. (a) How was heavenly direction of the congregation manifest in the first century? (b) What shows that Jesus is still the Head of the congregation?
7. (a) Who make up "the faithful and discreet slave," and why? (b) What assignment was given to the "slave"?

anointed congregation. Having purchased it with his blood, Jesus referred to it as his "slave." He commissioned its members to make disciples and to feed them progressively, giving them "their [spiritual] food at the proper time."—Matthew 24:45-47; 28:19; Isaiah 43:10; Luke 12:42; 1 Peter 4:10.

8 Since the slave class was loyally doing the Master's work at his invisible return in 1914, there is evidence that it was entrusted with enlarged responsibilities in 1919. The years since then have been the time for a global witness to the Kingdom, and a great crowd of worshipers of Jehovah is being gathered with a view to their preservation through the great tribulation. (Matthew 24:14, 21, 22; Revelation 7:9, 10) These too need spiritual food, and it is served to them by the slave class. To please Jehovah, we therefore need to accept the instruction he provides through this channel and to act in harmony with it.

9 At times, questions arise regarding doctrine and procedure. What then? Acts chapter 15 tells us how an issue regarding Gentile converts was resolved. The matter was referred to the apostles and older men at Jerusalem, who served as a central governing body. Those men were not infallible, but God used them. They considered the scriptures on the subject and also

---

8. (a) What responsibilities does the slave class now have? (b) Why is our response to instruction through God's channel important?

9, 10. (a) In the first century, what arrangement was there for resolving questions about doctrine and giving direction to preaching the good news? (b) What arrangement for coordinating the activities of Jehovah's people exists today?

the evidence of the operation of God's spirit in opening the Gentile field. Then they rendered a decision. God blessed that arrangement. (Acts 15:1-29; 16:4, 5) From that central body, individuals were sent out to further the Kingdom preaching.

10 In our day the Governing Body of Jehovah's visible organization is made up of spirit-anointed brothers from various lands and is located at the world headquarters of Jehovah's Witnesses. Under the headship of Jesus Christ, the Governing Body furthers pure worship in every land, coordinating the preaching activities of Jehovah's Witnesses in their tens of thousands of congregations. Those on the Governing Body share the viewpoint of the apostle Paul, who wrote to fellow Christians: "Not that we are the masters over your faith, but we are fellow workers for your joy, for it is by your faith that you are standing."—2 Corinthians 1:24.

11 Jehovah's Witnesses worldwide look to the Governing Body to select qualified brothers who, in turn, are authorized to appoint elders and ministerial servants to care for the congregations. The requirements for those appointed are stated in the Bible and take into account that those men are not perfect and make mistakes. The elders who make recommendations and those who do the appointing bear a serious responsibility before God. (1 Timothy 3:1-10, 12, 13; Titus 1:5-9) Hence, they offer prayer for the aid of God's spirit and seek guidance from his inspired Word. (Acts 6:

---

11. (a) How are elders and ministerial servants appointed? (b) Why should we cooperate closely with the appointed ones?

Jehovah guides us by means of his visible organization under Christ

2-4, 6; 14:23) Let us show our appreciation for these "gifts in men," who help us all attain to "the oneness in the faith."—Ephesians 4:8, 11-16.

12 The Scriptures direct that oversight in the congregation be cared for by men. This does not downgrade women, for some of them are heirs of the heavenly Kingdom, and they do much of the preaching work. (Psalm 68:11) Too, by faithfully caring for their family

---

12. How does Jehovah use women in the theocratic arrangement?

responsibilities, women contribute to the fine reputation of the congregation. (Titus 2:3-5) But teaching within the congregation is cared for by men who are appointed to do that.—1 Timothy 2:12, 13.

13 In the world, an individual who holds a prominent position is considered to be important, but within God's organization the rule is: "He that conducts himself as a lesser one among all of you is the one that is great." (Luke 9:46-48; 22:24-26) The Scriptures counsel elders to be careful not to lord it over those who are God's inheritance but, rather, to become examples to the flock. (1 Peter 5:2, 3) Not just a select few, but all of Jehovah's Witnesses, male and female, have the privilege of representing the Sovereign of the universe, humbly speaking in his name and telling people everywhere about his Kingdom.

14 We do well to ask ourselves: 'Do I truly appreciate how Jehovah is directing his visible organization? Do my attitudes, speech, and actions reflect that?' Reasoning on the following points can help each of us to make such an analysis.

If I truly submit to Christ as Head of the congregation, then, as indicated in the following scriptures, what will I be doing? (Matthew 24:14; 28:19, 20; John 13:34, 35)

When I appreciatively accept the spiritual provisions that come through the slave class and its Gov-

---

13. (a) What view does the Bible urge elders to take regarding their position? (b) In what privilege may all of us share?
14. Using the scriptures cited, discuss the questions listed at the end of the paragraph.

erning Body, for whom am I showing respect? (Luke 10:16)

How should everyone in the congregation, especially the elders, deal with one another? (Romans 12:10)

15 Jehovah is guiding us today by means of his visible organization under Christ. Our attitude toward this arrangement demonstrates how we feel about the issue of sovereignty. (Hebrews 13:17) Satan contends that our chief concern is self. But if we serve in any way needed and avoid things that draw undue attention to self, we prove the Devil a liar. If we love and respect those who take the lead among us but refuse to 'admire personalities for our own benefit,' we bring joy to Jehovah. (Jude 16; Hebrews 13:7) By being loyal to Jehovah's organization, we show that Jehovah is our God and that we are united in worship of him.—1 Corinthians 15:58.

---

15. (a) By our attitude toward Jehovah's visible organization, what do we demonstrate? (b) What opportunities are there for us to prove the Devil a liar and to bring joy to Jehovah's heart?

Review Discussion

- What is Jehovah's visible organization today? What is its purpose?
- Who is the appointed Head of the congregation, and through what visible arrangements does he provide loving direction for us?
- What wholesome attitudes should we cultivate toward those in Jehovah's organization?

CHAPTER FIFTEEN

Listen to Counsel, Accept Discipline

"WE ALL stumble many times," says the Bible at James 3:2. We can think of many instances where we have fallen short of being the sort of person God's Word urges us to be. So we acknowledge that the Bible is right when it says: "Listen to counsel and accept discipline, in order that you may become wise in your future." (Proverbs 19:20) No doubt we have already made adjustments in our lives to align them with the Bible's teachings. But how do we react if a fellow Christian counsels us on a specific matter?

2 Some react by trying to justify themselves, minimize the seriousness of the situation, or shift the blame to others. But it is better to listen to counsel and apply it. (Hebrews 12:11) Of course, no one should expect perfection of others, nor should he constantly give counsel about trivial things or on matters that the Bible leaves to personal choice. Too, perhaps the one giving counsel has not considered all the facts, and these may respectfully be called to his attention. But in the following discussion, let us assume that the counsel or discipline given is appropriate, Bible-based. How should one respond?

---

1. (a) Why do all of us need counsel and discipline? (b) What question do we need to consider?
2. What should we do when we receive personal counsel?

Examples for Our Admonition

3 God's Word contains real-life experiences of individuals who received needed counsel. At times, the counsel was accompanied by discipline. One such individual was King Saul of Israel. He failed to obey Jehovah regarding the nation of Amalek. The Amalekites had opposed God's servants, and Jehovah's divine judgment was that neither the Amalekites nor their livestock should be spared. But King Saul did spare their king and the best of their animals.—1 Samuel 15: 1-11.

4 Jehovah sent the prophet Samuel to reprove Saul. What was Saul's reaction? He argued that he did conquer the Amalekites but simply decided to spare their king. That, however, was contrary to Jehovah's command. (1 Samuel 15:20) Saul tried to shift the blame to the people for sparing the livestock, saying: "I feared the people and so obeyed their voice." (1 Samuel 15:24) He seemed more concerned with his pride, even asking Samuel to honor him in front of the people. (1 Samuel 15:30) Eventually, Jehovah rejected Saul as king. —1 Samuel 16:1.

5 King Uzziah of Judah "acted unfaithfully against Jehovah his God and came into the temple of Jehovah to burn incense." (2 Chronicles 26:16) But only priests could lawfully offer incense. When the chief priest tried to stop Uzziah, the king reacted with anger.

3, 4. (a) What does the Bible contain that can help us to develop the right view toward counsel and discipline? (b) How did King Saul react to counsel, and with what result?
5. What happened to King Uzziah when he rejected counsel?

What happened? The Bible says: "Leprosy itself flashed up in his forehead . . . because Jehovah had smitten him. And Uzziah the king continued to be a leper until the day of his death."—2 Chronicles 26:19-21.

6 Why did both Saul and Uzziah find it difficult to accept counsel? The basic problem was pride, each thinking too highly of himself. Many bring grief on themselves because of this trait. They seem to feel that acknowledging counsel implies some deficiency in them or hurts their reputation. But pride is a weakness. Pride beclouds a person's thinking so that he tends to resist the help provided by Jehovah through his Word and organization. Thus, Jehovah warns: "Pride is before a crash, and a haughty spirit before stumbling."—Proverbs 16:18; Romans 12:3.

Accepting Counsel

7 The Scriptures also contain fine examples of those who accepted counsel, and we can learn from these. Consider Moses, whose father-in-law gave him counsel on how to handle his heavy work load. Moses listened to him and immediately applied it. (Exodus 18:13-24) Although Moses had great authority, why was he receptive to counsel? Because he was humble. "Moses was by far the meekest of all the men who were upon the surface of the ground." (Numbers 12:3) How important is meekness? Zephaniah 2:3 shows that it means our life.

---

6. (a) Why did both Saul and Uzziah resist counsel? (b) Why is resisting counsel a serious problem today?
7. What positive lessons can be learned from the way Moses reacted to counsel?

8 King David committed adultery with Bath-sheba and tried to cover it up by having her husband, Uriah, killed. Jehovah sent the prophet Nathan to reprove David. He was repentant and quickly admitted: "I have sinned against Jehovah." (2 Samuel 12:13) While God accepted David's repentance, he would suffer the consequences of his wrongdoing. Jehovah told him that a sword would "not depart from [his] own house," that his wives would be given "to [his] fellowman," and that the son born from his adultery would "positively die." —2 Samuel 12:10, 11, 14.

9 King David knew the benefit of listening to sound counsel. On occasion, he thanked God for the one through whom it came. (1 Samuel 25:32-35) Are we like that? If so, we will be safeguarded against saying and doing many things that could cause regret. But what if we come into circumstances that lead to our being counseled or even disciplined? May we not forget that this is evidence of Jehovah's love, with our eternal welfare in view.—Proverbs 3:11, 12; 4:13.

Priceless Qualities to Cultivate

10 To have a good relationship with Jehovah and with our Christian brothers, we need to cultivate certain qualities. Jesus noted one of these when he set a child among his disciples and said: "Unless you turn around and become as young children, you will by no means

---

8. (a) What sins did David commit? (b) What was David's reaction to Nathan's reproof? (c) What were the consequences of David's sins?
9. What should we not forget if we are counseled or disciplined?
10. What quality did Jesus show was necessary for those who would get into the Kingdom?

enter into the kingdom of the heavens. Therefore, whoever will humble himself like this young child is the one that is the greatest in the kingdom of the heavens." (Matthew 18:3, 4) Jesus' disciples needed to cultivate humility, since they had argued among themselves as to who was the greatest.—Luke 22:24-27.

11 The apostle Peter wrote: "All of you gird yourselves with lowliness of mind toward one another, because God opposes the haughty ones, but he gives undeserved kindness to the humble ones." (1 Peter 5:5) We know that we need to be humble before God, but this scripture shows that we also need to be humble with fellow believers. If we are, we will not resent proper suggestions others offer us but will learn from them.—Proverbs 12:15.

12 Closely related to humility is concern for the welfare of others. The apostle Paul wrote: "Let each one keep seeking, not his own advantage, but that of the other person. . . . Therefore, whether you are eating or drinking or doing anything else, do all things for God's glory. Keep from becoming causes for stumbling to Jews as well as Greeks and to the congregation of God." (1 Corinthians 10:24-33) Paul did not say that we had to set aside all personal preferences, but he urged us not to do anything that might embolden someone else to do what his conscience told him was wrong.

---

11. (a) Before whom do we need to be humble, and why? (b) If we are humble, how will we respond to counsel?
12. (a) What important quality is closely related to humility? (b) Why should we be concerned about the effect that our conduct has on others?

13 Do you put the welfare of other people ahead of your own personal preference? All of us should learn to do that. There are many ways this can be done. Consider dress and grooming as an example. These are matters that involve personal taste within the Scriptural guidelines of being modest, neat, and clean. But if you were to learn that because of the background of people in your community, your manner of dress or grooming hindered others from listening to the Kingdom message, would you make adjustments? Surely, helping another person gain eternal life is more important than pleasing self.

14 In being humble and showing concern for others, Jesus set the example, even washing the feet of his disciples. (John 13:12-15) Of him, God's Word says: "Keep this mental attitude in you that was also in Christ Jesus, who, although he was existing in God's form, gave no consideration to a seizure, namely, that he should be equal to God. No, but he emptied himself and took a slave's form and came to be in the likeness of men. More than that, when he found himself in fashion as a man, he humbled himself and became obedient as far as death."–Philippians 2:5-8; Romans 15:2, 3.

Do Not Reject Jehovah's Discipline

15 Because we are all sinners, changes in our attitude

---

13. What example might indicate whether we make a practice of applying Scriptural counsel?
14. Why is it important to cultivate humility and concern for others?
15. (a) What changes do we need to make to have a personality that is pleasing to God? (b) By what means has Jehovah provided counsel and discipline for all of us?

and conduct are required if we are to reflect the personality of our God. We need to put on "the new personality." (Colossians 3:5-14) Counsel and discipline help us to identify areas where adjustments are needed and then to see how to make these. The basic source of the instruction we need is the Bible itself. (2 Timo-

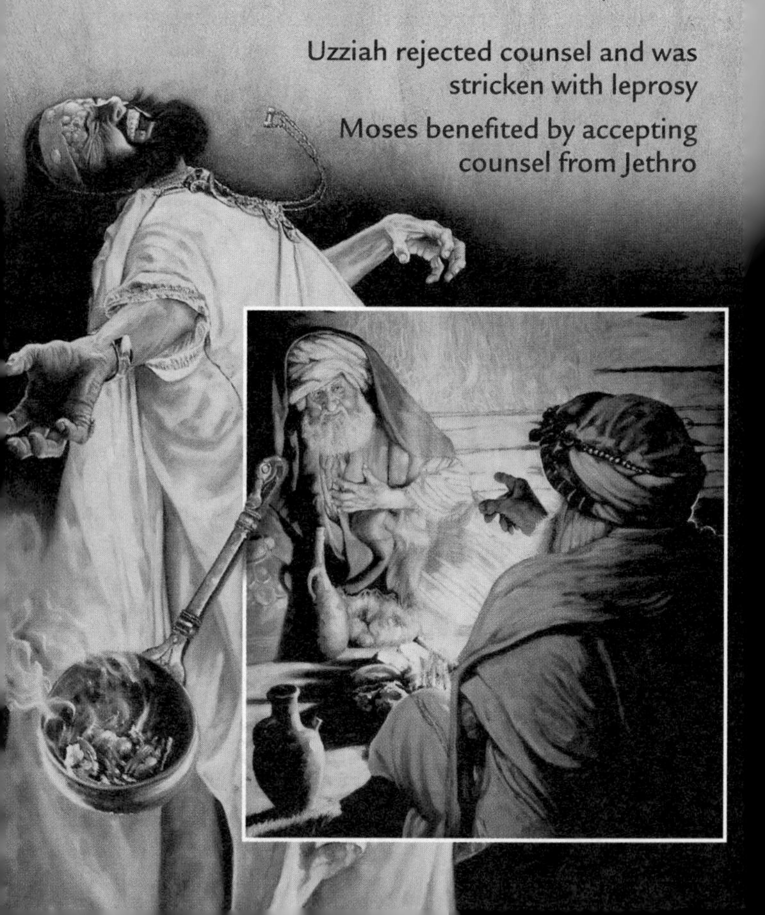

Uzziah rejected counsel and was stricken with leprosy

Moses benefited by accepting counsel from Jethro

thy 3:16, 17) Bible literature and meetings provided by Jehovah's organization help us to apply God's Word. Even if we have heard the counsel before, will we recognize our need for it and try to improve?

16 With loving concern, Jehovah helps us with our problems. Millions have been helped by means of home Bible studies. Parents counsel and discipline their children to safeguard them against conduct that could cause heartache. (Proverbs 6:20-23) Within the congregation, often some ask experienced ministers for counsel and suggestions so as to improve their own efforts in field activity. Elders may, at times, ask for counsel from one another or from others experienced in the ministry. Those with spiritual qualifications use the Bible to give assistance to those who need it, doing so in a spirit of mildness. If you give counsel, remember to "keep an eye on yourself, for fear you also may be tempted." (Galatians 6:1, 2) Yes, we all need counsel and discipline to worship the only true God unitedly.

---

16. What help does Jehovah provide for us as individuals?

Review Discussion

- How does Jehovah lovingly help us to see where we personally need to make adjustments?
- Why do many have difficulty in accepting needed counsel, and how serious is this?
- What priceless qualities will help us to be receptive to counsel, and how did Jesus set the example in these?

CHAPTER SIXTEEN

"Have Intense Love for One Another"

WHEN people first come to the meetings of Jehovah's Witnesses, they are often impressed by the love shown there. They observe it in the welcome extended to them and in the warm fellowship. Visitors to our conventions also notice this love. A news reporter wrote regarding a convention: 'Nobody under the influence of drugs or alcohol. No yelling and screaming. No pushing. No shoving. No one swearing or cursing. No dirty jokes or foul language. No smoke-filled air. No stealing. No one throwing cans on lawns. It was really unusual.' All of this is evidence of love, the kind that "does not behave indecently, does not look for its own interests."—1 Corinthians 13:4-8.

2 Brotherly love is the identifying mark of genuine Christians. (John 13:35) As we grow spiritually, we learn to express love more fully. The apostle Paul prayed that the love of his fellow Christians would "abound yet more and more." (Philippians 1:9) The apostle John showed that our love should be self-sacrificing. He wrote: "By this we have come to know

---

1. What often impresses newcomers at the meetings of Jehovah's Witnesses?

2. (a) In time, what should be evident as to our displaying love? (b) In imitation of Christ, what kind of love do we need to cultivate?

love, because [the Son of God] surrendered his soul for us; and we are under obligation to surrender our souls for our brothers." (1 John 3:16; John 15:12, 13) Would we actually give our life for our brothers? While most situations do not require that, to what extent do we go out of our way to help them now, even when it is not convenient?

3 Along with our deeds that reflect a self-sacrificing spirit, we need to have a genuinely warm feeling toward our brothers. God's Word urges us: "In brotherly love have tender affection for one another." (Romans 12:10) We all feel that way toward *some* people. But could we learn to feel such fondness for yet others? As the end of this old system draws near, it is vital for us to draw ever closer to our fellow Christians. The Bible says: "The end of all things has drawn close. . . . Above all things, have intense love for one another, because love covers a multitude of sins."—1 Peter 4:7, 8.

When Problems Arise

4 Of course, as long as we are imperfect, there will be times when we do things that offend others. Our brothers too may sin against us in various ways. (1 John 1:8) If you find yourself in such a situation, what should you do? The Scriptures provide the needed direction. But what they say may not coincide with what we as imperfect humans are inclined to do.

---

3. (a) In what way might we express our love more fully? (b) Why is it vital to have intense love for one another now?
4. (a) Why can problems arise between those in a congregation? (b) While we may not always be inclined to do so, what good can result if we apply the Bible's counsel?

(Romans 7:21-23) Nevertheless, our earnestly applying the counsel that the Bible contains will give evidence of our sincere desire to please Jehovah. Doing so will also enrich the quality of our love toward others.

5 When people are hurt, they sometimes look for ways to get even with the offender. But that only makes the situation worse. If recompense is needed, we should leave that to God. (Proverbs 24:29; Romans 12:17-21) Others may try to avoid contact with the offender. But we should not do that to fellow worshipers, for the acceptability of our own worship depends, in part, on our loving our brothers. (1 John 4:20) Thus, Paul wrote: "Continue putting up with one another and forgiving one another freely if anyone has a cause for complaint against another. Even as Jehovah freely forgave you, so do you also." (Colossians 3:13) Can you do that?

6 What if someone repeatedly sins against us but does not commit gross sins for which he can be put out of the congregation? For such lesser sins, the apostle Peter suggested forgiving "up to seven times." But Jesus said: "Not, Up to seven times, but, Up to seventy-seven times." He highlighted the enormity of our debt to God compared to what any human may owe us. (Matthew 18:21-35) In many ways we sin against God every day–sometimes by a selfish act, by what we say or think, or by what we fail to do–not even realizing that we are sinning. (Romans 3:23)

---

5. If someone hurts us, why should we not retaliate?
6. (a) How often should we forgive our brother? (b) Appreciating what will help us to handle a sin against us?

Yet, God continues to be merciful toward us. (Psalm 103:10-14; 130:3, 4) He requires us to deal the same way with one another. (Matthew 6:14, 15; Ephesians 4: 1-3) Then we will be practicing the kind of love that "does not keep account of the injury."—1 Corinthians 13:4, 5; 1 Peter 3:8, 9.

7 There may be times when we realize that even though we have no hard feelings toward our brother, he has something against us. We can choose to 'cover it over with love,' as 1 Peter 4:8 suggests. Or we can take the initiative to talk to him and try to restore peaceful relations.—Matthew 5:23, 24.

8 It could be that a fellow believer is doing something that upsets not only you but others too. Would it not be good to talk to him? Perhaps. If you personally explain the problem to him in a kind way, this may bring good results. But first you ought to ask yourself: 'Is he really doing something unscriptural? Or is the problem largely because my background and training are different from his?' Be careful not to set up your own standards and then judge according to these. (James 4:11, 12) Jehovah impartially accepts people from all sorts of backgrounds and is patient with them as they grow spiritually.

9 If someone in the congregation gets involved in

---

7. What should we do if a brother has something against us?

8. If a fellow believer does something that upsets us, what can be done about it?

9. (a) Who gives attention to cases of gross wrongdoing in the congregation? (b) When is it the responsibility of the one sinned against to act first, and with what objective?

Christian love is demonstrated in many ways, as at congregation meetings

gross wrongdoing, such as immorality, prompt attention should be given. By whom? By the elders. (James 5:14, 15) However, if a sin is committed against an individual, perhaps in a business matter or in the harmful misuse of the tongue, then the one sinned against should first endeavor to approach the offender on a private basis. (Matthew 18:15) If that does not resolve the matter, further steps need to be taken, as outlined at Matthew 18:16, 17. Love for our erring brother and a desire to 'gain' him will help us do this in a manner that seeks to reach his heart.—Proverbs 16:23.

10 When a problem comes up, whether it is great or

10. When a problem arises, what will help us to view the matter properly?

small, we are helped if we endeavor to understand how Jehovah views it. He does not approve of sin in any form, and in his due time, unrepentant practicers of gross sin are cleaned out of his organization. However, let us not forget that we all sin in lesser ways and are in need of his long-suffering and mercy. Jehovah thus sets a pattern to be imitated by us when we are confronted with the sins of others. When we are merciful, we are reflecting his love.—Ephesians 5:1, 2.

Seek Ways to "Widen Out"

11 Paul spent months building up the congregation in Corinth, Greece. He worked hard to help the brothers there, and he loved them. But some of them lacked warmth of feeling toward him. They were very critical. He urged them to "widen out" in expressing affection. (2 Corinthians 6:11-13; 12:15) We all do well to consider the extent to which we express love to others and to seek ways to widen out.—1 John 3:14.

12 Are there some in the congregation to whom we find it difficult to draw close? If we go out of our way to cover over any personality differences—as we would want them to do for us—this can help to warm the relationship between us. Our feelings toward them can also improve if we seek out their good qualities and concentrate on these. This will surely cause our love for them to grow.—Luke 6:32, 33, 36.

13 Admittedly, there are limitations to what we can

---

11. Why did Paul encourage the Corinthians to "widen out"?
12. How can we grow in our love for all in the congregation?
13. How can we widen out in showing love to those in our congregation?

do for others. We may not be able to greet everyone at each meeting. It may not be possible to include everyone when we invite friends for a meal. But could we widen out by spending just a few minutes getting better acquainted with someone in our congregation? Might we occasionally invite someone whom we do not know well to work with us in the field ministry?

14 Christian conventions afford fine opportunities to widen out in our love. Thousands may be present. We cannot meet them all, but we can conduct ourselves in a way that shows we put their welfare ahead of our convenience. Between sessions, we can show personal interest by taking the initiative to meet some of those around us. Someday all who live on earth will be brothers and sisters, united in worship of the true God and Father of all. What a joy it will be to get to know one another! Intense love will move us to want to do that. Why not start now?

---

14. When among Christians we have never met, how can we show intense love for one another?

Review Discussion

- When problems arise between Christians, how should these be resolved, and why?
- As we grow spiritually, in what ways should our love also grow?
- How is it possible to show intense love for more than just a close circle of friends?

CHAPTER SEVENTEEN

Practice Godly Devotion at Home

JEHOVAH is the Originator of marriage, and his Word provides the very best guidance for families. As a result of applying that guidance, many people have built successful marriages. Commendably, some who had merely lived together have been moved to register their marriage legally. Others have ceased having relationships outside of marriage. Violent men who were abusive to their wives and children have learned to show kindness and tenderness.

2 Christian family life involves many things, such as how we view the permanence of marriage, what we do to fulfill our responsibilities in the family, and how we deal with family members. (Ephesians 5:33–6:4) While we may know what the Bible says about family life, it is quite another thing to apply the Bible's counsel. None of us want to be like those whom Jesus condemned for sidestepping God's commandments. They falsely reasoned that mere religious devotion was enough. (Matthew 15:4-9) We do not want to have a form of godly devotion but fail to practice it in our own household. Rather, we want to display true godly devotion,

---

1. How has applying the guidance from God's Word affected marriages?

2. What is involved in Christian family life?

which is "a means of great gain."—1 Timothy 5:4; 6:6; 2 Timothy 3:5.

How Long Will the Marriage Last?

3 Increasingly, marriage bonds are proving to be fragile. Some couples who have been together for years decide to divorce and marry someone else. Also it is no longer unusual to hear that young couples have separated after being married for only a short time. Regardless of what others do, we should want to please Jehovah. So let us consider the following questions and scriptures to see what God's Word says about the permanence of marriage.

When a man and a woman marry, how long should they expect to stay together? (Mark 10:6-9; Romans 7:2, 3)

What is the only basis for divorce with the possibility of remarriage that is valid before God? (Matthew 5:31, 32; 19:3-9)

How does Jehovah feel about divorces that are not authorized by his Word? (Malachi 2:13-16)

Does the Bible advocate separation as a means to solve marital problems? (1 Corinthians 7:10-13)

Under what circumstances might a separation be warranted? (Psalm 11:5; Luke 4:8; 1 Timothy 5:8)

4 Some marriages are successful, lasting. Why? Waiting to marry until both parties are mature is a fac-

---

3. (a) What is happening to many marriages, but what should our determination be? (b) Using your Bible, answer the questions listed below this paragraph.
4. Why do some marriages endure?

tor, but finding a mate who shares one's interests and can discuss matters openly is also important. Of greater importance, though, is finding a mate who loves Jehovah and respects his Word as the basis for handling problems. (Psalm 119:97, 104; 2 Timothy 3:16, 17) Such a person will not have the attitude that if things do not work out, he can always get a separation or a divorce. He will not use his mate's shortcomings as an excuse to sidestep his own responsibilities. Instead, he will face up to problems and find workable solutions.

5 Satan contends that when we suffer, we will abandon Jehovah's ways. (Job 2:4, 5; Proverbs 27:11) But the vast majority of Jehovah's Witnesses who have suffered because of having an opposing mate have not renounced their marriage vows. They continue to be loyal to Jehovah and his commandments. (Matthew 5:37) Some who have persevered have had the joy of being joined by their mate in serving Jehovah—even after years of opposition! (1 Peter 3:1, 2) As for Christians whose mates show no signs of change or whose mates abandoned them because they serve Jehovah, these too know that they will be blessed for their giving evidence of godly devotion at home.—Psalm 55:22; 145:16.

Each One Doing His Part

6 Of course, having a successful marriage requires more than just staying together. A basic need on the

---

5. (a) How is loyalty to Jehovah involved in marriage? (b) Even when opposition is encountered, what benefits can come from holding to Jehovah's standards?

6. To have a successful marriage, what arrangement must be respected?

part of each mate is respect for Jehovah's arrangement of headship. This contributes to good order and a feeling of security in the home. At 1 Corinthians 11:3, we read: "The head of every man is the Christ; in turn the head of a woman is the man; in turn the head of the Christ is God."

7 Did you note what that verse mentioned first? Yes, every man has a Head, Christ, to whom he should submit. This means that the husband should exercise headship in a way that reflects the qualities of Jesus. Christ submits to Jehovah, deeply loves the congregation, and provides for it. (1 Timothy 3:15) He even "delivered up himself for it." Jesus is, not proud and inconsiderate, but "mild-tempered and lowly in heart." Those who come under his headship "find refreshment for [their] souls." When a husband deals with his family in this way, he shows that he is subjecting himself to Christ. A Christian wife should then find it beneficial and refreshing to cooperate with her husband and submit to his headship.—Ephesians 5:25-33; Matthew 11:28, 29; Proverbs 31:10, 28.

8 However, problems will arise. A measure of resentment at being directed by others may already have become deeply ingrained before anyone in the family began to apply Bible principles. Kind requests and a loving manner may not seem to get results. We know that the Bible says to put away "anger and

---

7. How should headship in the family be exercised?

8. (a) Why may it seem that Christian methods do not get the desired results in some homes? (b) What should we do if faced with such a situation?

wrath and screaming and abusive speech." (Ephesians 4:31) But if some do not seem to understand anything else, what should be done? Well, Jesus did not imitate those who threatened and reviled, but he relied on his Father. (1 Peter 2:22, 23) So when trying situations arise in the home, give evidence of godly devotion by praying to Jehovah for his help instead of adopting the ways of the world. —Proverbs 3:5-7.

A husband's headship should reflect the qualities of Jesus

9 Changes do not always come quickly, but Bible counsel really does work when applied patiently and diligently. Many husbands have found that the marriage began to improve when they came to appreciate Christ's dealings with the congregation. That congregation is not made up of perfect humans. Yet, Jesus loves it, sets the right example for it, and uses the Scriptures to help

9. Rather than finding fault, what have many Christian husbands learned to do?

it improve. He gave up his life in behalf of the congregation. (1 Peter 2:21) His example has encouraged many Christian husbands to provide good headship and offer loving help toward improvement. This yields much better results than does faultfinding or refusing to talk.

10 What if a husband is not sensitive to the emotional needs of his family or does not take the initiative to arrange for family discussion of the Bible and for other activities? Or what if a wife does not cooperate and show godly submissiveness? Some get good results by having respectful family discussions regarding problems. (Genesis 21:10-12; Proverbs 15:22) But even if the results are not all that were hoped for, each of us can contribute to an improved home atmosphere by making room for the fruitage of God's spirit in our life, showing loving consideration for other family members. (Galatians 5:22, 23) Progress will come, not by waiting for the other person to do something, but by doing our own part, thus showing that we practice godly devotion.—Colossians 3:18-21.

Where to Get Answers

11 There are many sources to which people turn for counsel on their family affairs. But we know that God's Word contains the very best advice, and we are grateful that through his visible organization, God

---

10. (a) In what ways might a husband or a wife—even one who professes to be a Christian—make life hard for others in the home? (b) What might be done to improve the situation?

11, 12. What has Jehovah provided to help us make a success of family life?

Having a regular Bible study with the family helps to unite it

helps us to apply it. Are you fully benefiting from that help?—Psalm 119:129, 130; Micah 4:2.

12 In addition to attending congregation meetings, have you set aside regular times for family Bible study? Families that do so can work toward being united in their worship. Their family life is enriched as they apply God's Word to their own circumstances.—Deuteronomy 11:18-21.

13 You may have questions on family matters. For example, what about birth control? Is abortion ever justified? If a child shows little interest in spiritual matters, to what extent should he be required to share in family worship? Many such questions have been discussed in the literature published by Jehovah's Witnesses. Learn to use Bible study aids, including indexes, to find the answers. If you do not have the publications referred to in an index, check the library at the Kingdom Hall. Or you may have access to these publications on your computer. You can also discuss your questions with mature Christian men and women. But do not always expect a yes or no answer to every question. Often *you* must decide, individually or as a married couple. Then make decisions that show that you practice godly devotion not only in public but also at home.—Romans 14:19; Ephesians 5:10.

---

13. (a) If we have questions on family matters, where can we often find the needed help? (b) What should be reflected in all decisions we make?

Review Discussion

- How is loyalty to Jehovah involved in faithfulness to one's marriage mate?
- When under pressure because of family problems, what will help us do what is pleasing to God?
- Even if others in the family fall short, what can we do to improve the situation?

CHAPTER EIGHTEEN

"They Are No Part of the World"

ON THE night before he was killed, Jesus prayed in behalf of his disciples. Knowing that they would be put under tremendous pressure by Satan, Jesus said to his Father: "I request you, not to take them out of the world, but to watch over them because of the wicked one. They are no part of the world, just as I am no part of the world." (John 17:15, 16) Why is separateness from the world so important? Because Satan is this world's ruler. Christians would not want to become part of a world that is under his control.—Luke 4:5-8; John 14:30; 1 John 5:19.

2 Being no part of the world did not mean that Jesus lacked love for others. On the contrary, he healed the sick, raised the dead, and taught people about God's Kingdom. He even gave his life for mankind. But he did not love the ungodly attitudes and actions of those who manifested the spirit of Satan's world. Thus, he warned against such things as immoral desires, a materialistic way of life, and grasping for prominence. (Matthew 5:27, 28; 6:19-21; Luke 20:46, 47) Not surprisingly, then, Jesus also avoided the world's politics. Although he was a Jew, he did not

---

1. (a) Before his death, what did Jesus pray in behalf of his disciples? (b) Why is being "no part of the world" so important?
2. In what ways was Jesus no part of the world?

take sides in the political controversies between Rome and the Jews.

"My Kingdom Is No Part of This World"

3 Consider what occurred when the Jewish religious leaders had Jesus arrested and taken to Pontius Pilate, the Roman governor. In reality, those leaders were disturbed because Jesus had exposed their hypocrisy. To get the governor to take action against Jesus, they accused him by saying: "This man we found subverting our nation and forbidding the paying of taxes to Caesar and saying he himself is Christ a king." (Luke 23:2) Clearly, this was a lie because a year earlier when the people wanted to make Jesus king, he refused. (John 6:15) He knew that he was to be a *heavenly* King in the future. (Luke 19:11, 12) Also, he was to be enthroned, not by humans, but by Jehovah.

4 Just three days before Jesus' arrest, the Pharisees tried to get Jesus to say something incriminating on the matter of paying taxes. But he said: "Show me a denarius [a Roman coin]. Whose image and inscription does it have?" When they said "Caesar's," he replied: "By all means, then, pay back Caesar's things to Caesar, but God's things to God."—Luke 20:20-25.

5 No, Jesus did not teach rebellion against secular

---

3. (a) What accusation regarding Jesus did Jewish religious leaders make to Pilate, and why? (b) What shows that Jesus had no interest in becoming a human king?
4. What was Jesus' attitude toward the paying of taxes?
5. (a) What lesson did Jesus teach his disciples at the time of his arrest? (b) How did Jesus explain the reason for what he had done? (c) What was the outcome of that trial?

authorities. When soldiers and other men came to arrest Jesus, Peter drew a sword and struck one of the men, cutting off an ear. But Jesus said: "Return your sword to its place, for all those who take the sword will perish by the sword." (Matthew 26:51, 52) The next day Jesus explained his actions to Pilate, saying: "My kingdom is no part of this world. If my kingdom were part of this world, my attendants would have fought that I should not be delivered up to the Jews." (John 18:36) Pilate admitted that there was "no ground for the charges" against Jesus. But bowing to pressure from the mob, Pilate had Jesus impaled. —Luke 23:13-15; John 19:12-16.

Disciples Follow Jesus' Lead

6 The disciples of Jesus thus understood what being no part of the world required. It meant avoiding the ungodly spirit and actions of the world, which included the violent and immoral entertainment of the Roman circus and theater. For that, the disciples were called haters of mankind. But far from hating their fellowmen, they worked hard to help others benefit from God's provisions for salvation.

7 The followers of Jesus were persecuted as he had been, often by misinformed government officials. Yet, about 56 C.E., the apostle Paul wrote to Christians in Rome, urging them to "be in subjection to

---

6. How did the early Christians show that they avoided the spirit of the world but loved people?
7. (a) Because of being no part of the world, what did the early disciples experience? (b) How did they view the political rulers and the paying of taxes, and why?

the superior authorities [political rulers], for there is no authority except by God." Not that Jehovah establishes secular governments, but he allows them to exist until his Kingdom alone rules all the earth. Appropriately, Paul advised Christians to respect secular officials and to pay taxes.—Romans 13:1-7; Titus 3: 1, 2.

8 However, subjection to political rulers is to be *relative,* not unlimited. When there is a conflict between Jehovah's laws and man's laws, those who serve Jehovah are to obey His laws. Notice what the book *On the Road to Civilization—A World History* says of the early Christians: "Christians refused to share certain duties of Roman citizens. The Christians . . . felt it a violation of their faith to enter military service. They would not hold political office. They would not worship the emperor." When the Jewish high court "positively ordered" the disciples to stop preaching, they answered: "We must obey God as ruler rather than men."—Acts 5:27-29.

9 Regarding political and military controversies, the disciples maintained strict neutrality. In 66 C.E., the Jews in Judea revolted against Caesar. The Roman army quickly surrounded Jerusalem. What did Christians in the city do? They remembered Jesus' counsel to get out of the city. When the Romans temporarily

---

8. (a) To what extent are Christians to be in subjection to the superior authorities? (b) How did the early Christians follow Jesus' example?

9. (a) Why did Christians in Jerusalem take the action they did in 66 C.E.? (b) In what way is that a valuable pattern?

withdrew, the Christians fled across the Jordan River into the mountainous region of Pella. (Luke 21:20-24) Their neutrality serves as a pattern for faithful Christians later.

Christian Neutrals in These Last Days

10 Does the historical record show that any group in these last days has pursued strict neutrality in imitation of the early Christians? Yes, Jehovah's Witnesses have done so. All during this time period, they have kept preaching that God's Kingdom is the only means to bring lasting peace, prosperity, and happiness to lovers of righteousness. (Matthew 24:14) But with regard to controversies among the nations, they have maintained strict neutrality.

11 In sharp contrast, the clergy of this world's religions have been very involved in political affairs. In some lands, they have actively campaigned for or against candidates. Some of the clergy even hold political office. Others have pressured politicians to favor programs that the clergy approve. However, Jehovah's Witnesses do not meddle in politics. Nor do they interfere with what others do as to joining a political party, running for political office, or voting in elections. Jesus said that his disciples would be no part of the world, so Jehovah's Witnesses take no part in politics.

---

10. (a) In what work do Jehovah's Witnesses keep busy, and why? (b) Regarding what are they neutral?
11. (a) How does the neutrality of the Witnesses contrast with the practices of the clergy? (b) What view do Jehovah's Witnesses take regarding what others do about politics?

12 As Jesus foretold, nations have repeatedly gone to war. Even factions within nations have fought one another. (Matthew 24:3, 6, 7) The religious leaders have almost always supported one nation or faction against another, urging their followers to do the same. The result? Members of the same religion kill one another in battle just because of differences in nationality or tribe. This is contrary to God's will. —1 John 3:10-12; 4:8, 20.

13 However, Jehovah's Witnesses have been strictly neutral in all conflicts. *The Watchtower* of November 1, 1939, stated: "All who are on the Lord's side will be neutral as to warring nations." Jehovah's Witnesses in all nations and under all circumstances continue to hold to this position. They do not allow the world's divisive politics and wars to break up their international brotherhood. They "beat their swords into plowshares and their spears into pruning shears." Being neutral, they do not learn war anymore.—Isaiah 2:3, 4; 2 Corinthians 10:3, 4.

14 What is one result of their neutrality? Jesus said: "Because you are no part of the world, . . . the world hates you." (John 15:19) Many of Jehovah's Witnesses have been imprisoned because of being God's servants. Some have been tortured, even killed, similar to what happened to first-century Christians. This is

---

12. What has resulted because the religions of this world are not neutral?
13. What do the facts show about the neutrality of Jehovah's Witnesses?
14. Because of maintaining separateness from the world, what have Jehovah's Witnesses experienced?

Jesus explained that he and his followers were "no part of the world"

because Satan, "the god of this system of things," opposes Jehovah's servants, who are no part of it.—2 Corinthians 4:4; Revelation 12:12.

15 Jehovah's servants are happy that they are no part of the world, for all of its nations are marching to their end at Armageddon. (Daniel 2:44; Revelation 16:14, 16; 19:11-21) We will avoid that fate because we stand apart from the world. As a united people earth wide, we are loyal to God's heavenly Kingdom. True, by being no part of the world, we are exposed to its ridicule and persecution. Very soon, though, that will stop, since this present evil world under Satan will be destroyed forever. On the other hand, those who serve Jehovah will live forever in his righteous new world under God's Kingdom.—2 Peter 3:10-13; 1 John 2:15-17.

---

15. (a) To what are all nations marching, and what are Jehovah's Witnesses careful to avoid? (b) Why is separateness from the world such a serious matter?

Review Discussion

- How did Jesus show what is involved in being "no part of the world"?
- What was the attitude of the early Christians toward (a) the spirit of the world, (b) secular rulers, and (c) the paying of taxes?
- In what ways have Jehovah's Witnesses in modern times given evidence of their Christian neutrality?

CHAPTER NINETEEN

Continue to Speak God's Word With Boldness

NEARLY 2,000 years ago, God's Son, Jesus Christ, was anointed as the future King over all the earth. Jesus was executed at the instigation of religious enemies, but Jehovah raised him from the dead. Through Jesus, everlasting life was now possible. When Jesus' disciples publicly proclaimed this good news, however, persecution broke out. Some of them were thrown into prison, even flogged and ordered to stop speaking about Jesus. (Acts 4:1-3, 17; 5:17, 18, 40) What would they do? What would you have done? Would you have continued to witness boldly?

2 In 1914 the King of God's Kingdom, Jesus Christ, was enthroned in heaven to rule 'in the midst of his enemies.' (Psalm 110:2) Next, Satan and his demons were hurled down to the earth. (Revelation 12:1-5, 7-12) The last days of the present wicked system had begun. When this time period ends, God will crush the entire satanic system of things. (Daniel 2:44; Matthew 24:21) Survivors will have before them the prospect of everlasting life on an earth that will become a paradise. If you have embraced this good news, you

---

1. (a) What good news did Jesus' disciples proclaim, but how did some of the Jews react? (b) What questions might we ask?
2. (a) What marvelous news needs to be proclaimed in our day? (b) Who have the responsibility to preach the good news?

will want to share it with others. (Matthew 24:14) But what response can you expect?

3 When you proclaim the Kingdom good news, some people may welcome it, but most will be indifferent. (Matthew 24:37-39) Some may ridicule or oppose you. Jesus warned that opposition might come from your own relatives. (Luke 21:16-19) It may also come at your place of work or at school. In some parts of the earth, Jehovah's Witnesses are even under governmental ban. When confronted with such circumstances, will you continue to speak God's word boldly and "stand firm in the faith"?—1 Corinthians 16:13.

Not Relying on Our Own Strength

4 Basic to being a faithful servant of Jehovah is reliance on his provisions. One of these is congregation meetings. The Scriptures urge us not to neglect them. (Hebrews 10:23-25) Those who have continued to be faithful Witnesses of Jehovah have exerted themselves to be regular in attendance at meetings with fellow worshipers. At these meetings our knowledge of the Scriptures is increased. Also, our appreciation of well-known truths grows, and our awareness of ways in which to use them is sharpened. We are drawn closer to our Christian brothers in united worship and are strengthened to do God's will. Jehovah's spirit provides direction through the congregation, and by

---

3. (a) How do people respond to the Kingdom message? (b) What question must we face?

4. (a) To prove ourselves faithful servants of God, what is a basic requirement? (b) Why are Christian meetings so important?

means of that spirit, Jesus is in our midst.—Matthew 18:20; Revelation 3:6.

5 Do you regularly attend all the meetings, and do you make personal application of what you hear discussed? Sometimes, when Jehovah's Witnesses are under ban, it is necessary to hold the meetings in small groups in private homes. Places and times may vary and may not always be convenient, some meetings being held late at night. But in spite of personal inconvenience or danger, faithful brothers and sisters put forth earnest effort to be present for each meeting.

6 Reliance on Jehovah is developed by regularly turning to him in heartfelt prayer, realizing that we need God's help. Do you do that? Jesus prayed repeatedly during his earthly ministry. (Luke 3:21; 6:12, 13; 22:39-44) And on the night before his impalement, he urged his disciples: "Keep on the watch and praying, in order that you do not come into temptation." (Mark 14:38) If we encounter indifference to the Kingdom message, we could be tempted to slow down in our ministry. If people ridicule us or persecute us, we might feel tempted to keep quiet to avoid problems. But if we pray earnestly for God's spirit to help us to keep on speaking boldly, we will be safeguarded against giving in to those temptations. —Luke 11:13; Ephesians 6:18-20.

---

5. When Jehovah's Witnesses are under ban, what is done about meetings?

6. How do we demonstrate our reliance on Jehovah, and how can this help us to keep on speaking boldly?

A Record of Bold Witnessing

7 The record contained in the book of Acts is of special interest to all of us. It tells how the apostles and other early disciples—people who had feelings like ours—overcame obstacles and proved to be bold and faithful witnesses of Jehovah. Let us examine a portion of that record with the aid of the following questions and cited scriptures. As we do so, consider how you can personally benefit from what you are reading.

Were the apostles highly educated men? Were they individuals who by nature were fearless, regardless of what happened? (John 18:17, 25-27; 20:19; Acts 4:13)

What enabled Peter to speak boldly before the Jewish court that had condemned God's own Son? (Matthew 10:19, 20; Acts 4:8)

What had the apostles been doing during the weeks before they were brought before the Sanhedrin? (Acts 1:14; 2:1, 42)

When the rulers ordered the apostles to stop preaching on the basis of Jesus' name, how did Peter and John reply? (Acts 4:19, 20)

After their release, to whom did the apostles again look for help? Did they pray for the persecution to stop, or what? (Acts 4:24-31)

By what means did Jehovah provide assistance when opposers tried to stop the preaching work? (Acts 5:17-20)

---

7. (a) Why is the record in Acts of special interest to us? (b) Answer the questions provided at the end of this paragraph, emphasizing how the information can benefit us.

How did the apostles show that they understood the reason why they had been delivered? (Acts 5:21, 41, 42)

Even when many of the disciples were scattered because of persecution, what did they continue to do? (Acts 8:3, 4; 11:19-21)

8 The work of preaching the good news was not in vain. About 3,000 disciples were baptized at Pentecost 33 C.E. "Believers in the Lord kept on being added, multitudes both of men and of women." (Acts 2: 41; 4:4; 5:14) In time, even a fierce persecutor of God's people, Saul of Tarsus, became a Christian and boldly began witnessing to the truth. He came to be known as the apostle Paul. (Galatians 1:22-24) The work that began in the first century has not stopped. It has gathered momentum in these last days and has reached all parts of the earth. We have the privilege of sharing in it, and as we do so, we can learn from the example set by loyal witnesses who served before us.

9 When Paul learned the truth about Jesus Christ, what did he do? "Immediately . . . he began to preach Jesus, that this One is the Son of God." (Acts 9:20) He appreciated God's undeserved kindness to him, and he realized that everyone needed the good news that he had received. Paul was a Jew, and according to

---

8. What thrilling results came from the ministry of the early disciples, and how have we come to be involved?

9. (a) What opportunities did Paul use to witness? (b) In what ways do you spread the Kingdom message to others?

the custom of the day, he went to the synagogues to give a witness. He also preached from house to house and reasoned with people in the marketplace. And he was willing to move into new territories to preach the good news.—Acts 17:17; 20:20; Romans 15:23, 24.

10 Paul was bold but also discerning, as we should be. To Jews he appealed on the basis of the promises made by God to their forefathers. To Greeks he spoke on the basis of things with which they were familiar. At times he used his own experience in learning the truth as a vehicle for giving a witness. He said: "I do all things for the sake of the good news, that I may become a sharer of it with others."—1 Corinthians 9:20-23; Acts 22:3-21.

11 When opposition made it seem better for Paul to preach in another area for a time, he did so instead of forcing repeated confrontations with opposers. (Acts 14:5-7; 18:5-7; Romans 12:18) But he was never ashamed of the good news. (Romans 1:16) Though Paul found the insolent—even violent—treatment by opposers unpleasant, he "mustered up boldness by means of our God" to keep on preaching. He said: "The Lord stood near me and infused power into me,

---

10. (a) How did Paul show that while bold, he was also discerning in the way he witnessed? (b) How might we reflect Paul's qualities when witnessing to relatives, workmates, or schoolmates?

11. (a) What did Paul do to avoid repeated confrontations with opposers? (b) When might we wisely imitate Paul's example, and how? (c) From where does the power come to keep on speaking boldly?

As in the past, Jehovah's servants today speak God's word with boldness

that through me the preaching might be fully accomplished." (1 Thessalonians 2:2; 2 Timothy 4:17) The Head of the Christian congregation, Jesus, continues to provide the power we need to do the work he foretold for our day.—Mark 13:10.

12 We have every reason to continue speaking God's word boldly, just as Jesus and other faithful servants of God did in the first century. This does not mean being inconsiderate or trying to force the message on those who do not want it. But we do not give up because people are indifferent; nor are we silenced by opposition. Like Jesus, we point to God's Kingdom as the rightful government of all the earth. We speak with confidence because we represent Jehovah, the Universal Sovereign, and because the message we proclaim is not from us but from him. And our love for Jehovah should be our strongest motive for praising him.—Philippians 1:27, 28; 1 Thessalonians 2:13.

---

12. What gives evidence of Christian boldness, and what is the basis for it?

Review Discussion

- Why is it important to share the Kingdom message with everyone possible, but what reactions can we expect?
- How can we show that we do not rely on our own strength to serve Jehovah?
- What valuable lessons do we learn from the book of Acts?

CHAPTER TWENTY

Keep Close in Mind Jehovah's Day

ONE of the first things you learned from the Bible was that Jehovah's purpose is for all the earth to become a paradise. In that new world, war, crime, poverty, sickness, suffering, and death will be no more. Even the dead will come back to life. What marvelous prospects! The nearness of all that is emphasized by evidence that Christ's invisible presence as ruling King began in 1914 and that since then we have been in the last days of this wicked world. At the end of these last days, Jehovah will destroy this present system of things and usher in the promised new world!

2 The Bible calls this coming time of destruction "Jehovah's day." (2 Peter 3:10) It is "the day of Jehovah's anger" against Satan's entire world. (Zephaniah 2:3) It reaches its climax in "the war of the great day of God the Almighty . . . , called in Hebrew Har–Magedon [Armageddon]," in which "the kings of the entire inhabited earth" are annihilated. (Revelation 16:14, 16) Does your way of life demonstrate your conviction that this "day of Jehovah" is near?—Zephaniah 1:14-18; Jeremiah 25:33.

---

1. When you first learned that deliverance from the heartaches of this old system is near, how did you feel?
2. What is "the day of Jehovah"?

3 The Bible does not tell us the exact date when Jesus Christ will come as Jehovah's Executioner against Satan's system of things. "Concerning that day or the hour nobody knows, neither the angels in heaven nor the Son, but the Father," said Jesus. (Mark 13:32) If any do not really love Jehovah, they will be inclined to postpone his day in their minds and turn to secular pursuits. But those who truly love Jehovah will serve him whole-souled, regardless of when the end of this wicked system comes.—Psalm 37:4; 1 John 5:3.

4 In a word of caution to lovers of Jehovah, Jesus says: "Keep looking, keep awake, for you do not know when the appointed time is." (Mark 13:33-37) He urges us not to allow eating and drinking or "anxieties of life" to absorb so much of our attention that we lose sight of the seriousness of the times.—Luke 21:34-36; Matthew 24:37-42.

5 Peter similarly counsels us to keep close in mind "the presence of the day of Jehovah, through which the heavens being on fire will be dissolved and the elements being intensely hot will melt." All human governments—"the heavens"—will be destroyed, as will wicked human society in general—"earth"—and its "elements," the ideas and activities of this evil world, such as its attitude of independence from God and its immoral and materialistic way of life. These will

---

3. (a) When will the day of Jehovah come? (b) How has it proved beneficial that Jehovah did not reveal "that day or the hour"?
4. What did Jesus say as a caution?
5. As Peter explained, what will the day of Jehovah bring?

be replaced by a "new heavens [God's heavenly Kingdom] and a new earth [a new earthly society]" in which "righteousness is to dwell." (2 Peter 3:10-13) These world-shattering events will begin suddenly and at an unexpected day and hour.—Matthew 24:44.

Keep Alert to the Sign

6 In view of the times in which we live, we should become well acquainted with the details of the composite sign that identifies the last days—"the conclusion of the system of things." Keep in mind that when Jesus answered his disciples' question, recorded at Matthew 24:3, some of what he described in verses 4 through 22 had a small-scale fulfillment on the Jewish system between 33 and 70 C.E. But the prophecy has its major fulfillment in the period since 1914, the time of Christ's "presence and of the conclusion of the system of things." Matthew 24:23-28 tells what would take place from 70 C.E. to the time of Christ's presence. The developments described at Matthew 24:29–25:46 take place during the time of the end.

7 We personally ought to be observant of events and attitudes that fulfill the sign. Connecting these things to Bible prophecy will help us to keep close in mind Jehovah's day. It will also enable us to be persuasive

---

6. (a) To what extent did Jesus' answer to his disciples' question apply to the end of the Jewish system? (b) What portions of Jesus' answer focus attention on events and attitudes from 1914 onward?

7. (a) Why should we personally be alert to how current conditions fulfill the sign? (b) Answer the questions at the end of this paragraph, showing how the sign has been fulfilled since 1914.

when warning others of the nearness of that day. (Isaiah 61:1, 2) With these objectives in mind, let us review the following questions that highlight parts of the sign, as recorded at Matthew 24:7 and Luke 21: 10, 11.

In what extraordinary way was the foretold rising of 'nation against nation and kingdom against kingdom' fulfilled starting in 1914? Regarding wars, what has happened since then?

In 1918, what pestilence claimed more lives than World War I? Despite man's medical knowledge, what diseases still kill millions?

To what extent have food shortages affected the earth despite the scientific advances of the last century?

What convinces you that 2 Timothy 3:1-5, 13 is describing, not the way that life has always been, but the way that bad conditions have intensified as we move toward the end of the last days?

Separating of People

8 There are other significant developments that Jesus associated with the conclusion of the system of things. One of these is the separating of "the sons of the kingdom" from "the sons of the wicked one." Jesus spoke of this in his parable about a wheat field that an enemy oversowed with weeds. "The wheat" in

---

8. (a) What else, described at Matthew 13:24-30, 36-43, did Jesus associate with the conclusion of the system of things? (b) What does Jesus' illustration mean?

his illustration represents true anointed Christians. "The weeds" are those who profess to be Christians but prove themselves to be "sons of the wicked one" because they cling to the world of which the Devil is ruler. These are separated from "the sons of [God's] kingdom" and are marked for destruction. (Matthew 13:24-30, 36-43) Has this actually taken place?

9 After World War I, there was a separating of all who claimed to be Christian into two classes: (1) The clergy of Christendom and their followers, who came out in strong support of the League of Nations (now the United Nations) while still holding fast to their national loyalties, and (2) true Christians of that postwar era, who gave their full support to God's Messianic Kingdom, not to the nations of this world. (John 17:16) These proved themselves true servants of God's Kingdom by undertaking the preaching of "this good news of the kingdom" earth wide. (Matthew 24:14) With what results?

10 First, there was the gathering of the remnant of those anointed by God's spirit, who have the hope of being with Christ as part of the heavenly Kingdom. Though such ones were scattered among the nations, they were brought into organizational unity. The completion of the sealing of these anointed ones draws near.—Revelation 7:3, 4.

---

9. (a) After World War I, what great separation of all claiming to be Christian took place? (b) How did anointed Christians give evidence that they were true servants of the Kingdom?

10. What was the first result of the Kingdom-preaching activity?

11 Then, under Christ's direction, there began the gathering of "a great crowd . . . out of all nations and tribes and peoples and tongues." These make up the "other sheep" who will survive "the great tribulation" into God's new world. (Revelation 7:9, 14; John 10: 16) This work of preaching God's Kingdom before the end comes continues right down to the present time.

11. (a) What gathering work continues, and in harmony with what prophecy? (b) What does fulfillment of this prophecy signify?

Soon the last days will end with the destruction of Satan's system

Loyally, the great crowd of other sheep, now numbering into the millions, help the anointed remnant publicize the vital message of the Kingdom. This message is being heard in all nations.

What Lies Ahead?

12 All of the above signifies that we are near the end of the last days and that Jehovah's day is close at hand. But are there prophecies yet to be fulfilled before that fear-inspiring day begins? Yes. For one

---

12. How much more preaching work is to be done before Jehovah's day arrives?

thing, the separating of people over the Kingdom issue is not yet finished. In some areas where intense opposition was experienced for years, there is now an increase in new disciples. Even where people reject the good news, Jehovah's mercy is demonstrated by our giving the witness. So, on with the work! Jesus assures us that when the work is finished, the end will come.

13 Another highly significant Bible prophecy foretells: "Whenever it is that they are saying: 'Peace and security!' then sudden destruction is to be instantly upon them just as the pang of distress upon a pregnant woman; and they will by no means escape." (1 Thessalonians 5:2, 3) What form that proclamation of "peace and security" will take remains to be seen. But it will certainly not mean that world leaders have truly solved the problems of mankind. Those who are keeping Jehovah's day close in mind will not be misled by that proclamation. They know that immediately afterward, sudden destruction will come.

14 At the beginning of the great tribulation, the rulers will turn against Babylon the Great, the world empire of false religion, and will annihilate her. (Matthew 24:21; Revelation 17:15, 16) After that, the nations will turn against those who uphold Jehovah's sovereignty, provoking Jehovah's fury against the po-

---

13. As recorded at 1 Thessalonians 5:2, 3, what noteworthy event is yet to take place, and what will it mean to us?
14. What events will take place during the great tribulation, and in what order?

litical governments and their supporters, resulting in total destruction for them. That will be the Armageddon climax of the great tribulation. Then, Satan and his demons will be abyssed, no longer able to influence mankind. This will conclude Jehovah's day when his name will be put on high.—Ezekiel 38:18, 22, 23; Revelation 19:11–20:3.

15 The end of this system will come exactly on time, according to God's schedule. It will not be late. (Habakkuk 2:3) Remember, the destruction of Jerusalem in 70 C.E. came quickly, when the Jews did not expect it, when they thought that danger was past. And what of ancient Babylon? It was powerful, confident, and fortified with massive walls. But it fell in one night. So, too, sudden destruction will come upon the present wicked system. When it does, may we be found united in true worship, having kept close in mind Jehovah's day.

---

15. Why would it be unwise to reason that Jehovah's day is yet far off?

Review Discussion

- Why is it vital to keep close in mind Jehovah's day? How can we do that?
- How are we personally affected by the separating of people that is taking place?
- What still lies ahead before Jehovah's day begins? So, what should we personally be doing?

CHAPTER TWENTY-ONE

Jehovah's Purpose Attains Glorious Success

ALL intelligent creation united in worshiping the only true God and all of them enjoying glorious freedom as children of God—that is Jehovah's loving purpose. It is also what lovers of righteousness earnestly desire.

2 Jehovah began fulfilling this grand purpose when he started his works of creation. His first creation was a Son who since his resurrection is "the reflection of [God's] glory and the exact representation of his very being." (Hebrews 1:1-3) This Son was unique, being created by God alone. Subsequently, it would be through this Son that all others were to be brought into existence: first the angels in heaven, then humans on earth. (Job 38:7; Luke 3:38) All of these made up one universal family. To all of them, Jehovah was God, the Universal Sovereign, and their loving Father.

3 When our first human parents were condemned to death as willful sinners, they were evicted from Eden and disowned by God. They ceased to be part of his universal family. (Genesis 3:22-24; Deuteronomy 32:

1, 2. (a) What is Jehovah's purpose regarding his intelligent creatures? (b) Who were included in God's united family of worshipers?
3. (a) What have all of us inherited from our first parents? (b) What loving provision did Jehovah make for Adam's offspring?

4, 5) All of us are their descendants, so we have been born with sinful tendencies. But Jehovah knew that some from among Adam and Eve's descendants would love righteousness. So He lovingly made a provision whereby these could attain to "the glorious freedom of the children of God."—Romans 8:20, 21.

Israel Loses Favored Position

4 Some 2,500 years after Adam's creation, Jehovah extended to certain humans the privilege of having a special relationship with Him. He chose ancient Israel to be his people and gave them his Law. (Genesis 12: 1, 2) He formed them into a nation and used them in connection with his purpose. (Deuteronomy 14:1, 2; Isaiah 43:1) However, they were still in bondage to sin and death, so they did not enjoy the glorious freedom that Adam and Eve originally had.

5 Nevertheless, the Israelites had a favored standing with God. They also had the responsibility to respect Jehovah as their Father and to work in harmony with his purpose. Jesus stressed the importance of their fulfilling that obligation. (Matthew 5:43-48) However, the nation of Israel failed to do this. While those Jews claimed "we have one Father, God," Jesus declared that their actions and the spirit they showed belied such a claim. (John 8:41, 44, 47) In 33 C.E., the Law was terminated by God, and Israel's special relationship with him ended. But did this mean that people could never enjoy a favorable relationship with God?

---

4. What privilege did Jehovah extend to ancient Israel?
5. How did the Israelites lose their special standing with God?

Gathering "the Things in the Heavens"

6 The apostle Paul showed that some among humankind could enjoy a special relationship with God. For example, regarding Jehovah's arrangement whereby those who exercise faith may become members of His household, Paul wrote: "[God] made known to us the sacred secret of his will. It is according to his good pleasure which he purposed in himself for an administration at the full limit of the appointed times, namely, to gather all things together again in the Christ, the things in the heavens and the things on the earth." (Ephesians 1:9, 10) This "administration" centers on Jesus Christ. Through him, humans are brought into an approved condition before God. A limited number of them have the prospect of being in heaven. Far greater numbers will live on earth forever.

7 First, starting in Pentecost 33 C.E., attention was given to "the things in the heavens," that is, those who would be joint heirs with Christ in the heavenly Kingdom. On the basis of their faith in the value of Jesus' sacrifice, they were declared righteous by God. (Romans 5:1, 2) In time, Jews and Gentiles were included, and "the things in the heavens" would number 144,000. (Galatians 3:26-29; Revelation 14:1) Only a remnant of them are still on earth.

Gathering "the Things on the Earth"

8 The same administration is also gathering "the

---

6. What is the purpose of the "administration" that Paul mentioned at Ephesians 1:9, 10?
7. Who are "the things in the heavens"?
8. Who are "the things on the earth," and what is their relationship with Jehovah?

things on the earth." Millions of people are now being gathered with the prospect of living forever on earth. In unity with the remnant of Kingdom heirs, they magnify the name of Jehovah and exalt his worship. (Isaiah 2:2, 3; Zephaniah 3:9) They also address Jehovah as "Father" because they recognize him as the source of life. And they enjoy an approved standing before him on the basis of their faith in Jesus' shed blood. (Revelation 7:9, 14) But since they are still imperfect, being fully acknowledged as God's children is yet future.

9 These with earthly hopes are now eagerly waiting for the time when the human creation will be "set free from enslavement to corruption." (Romans 8:21) That emancipation will begin after Christ and his heavenly armies bring the great tribulation to a close by means of the Armageddon climax. This will mean the destruction of Satan's entire wicked system of things, to be followed by the blessings of the Thousand Year Reign of Christ in Kingdom power.—Revelation 19:17-21; 20:6.

10 How exhilarating it will be when Jehovah's servants on earth unite to echo the sentiments of his servants in heaven, who joyously proclaim: "Great and wonderful are your works, Jehovah God, the Almighty. Righteous and true are your ways, King of eternity. Who will not really fear you, Jehovah, and glorify your name, because you alone are loyal? For all the nations will come and worship before you, because

---

9. What promise does Romans 8:21 hold out for mankind?
10. Jehovah's servants will sing what song of praise?

your righteous decrees have been made manifest." (Revelation 15:3, 4) Yes, all of Jehovah's servants will unite in worship of the only true God. Even the dead will be resurrected and given the opportunity to join in raising their voices in praise to Jehovah.—Acts 24:15.

Marvelous Freedom Ahead

11 After the great tribulation, with its Armageddon climax, has cleansed the earth of wickedness, no longer will Satan the Devil be "the god of this system of things." No longer will worshipers of Jehovah have to contend with Satan's vile influence. (2 Corinthians 4:4; Revelation 20:1, 2) No longer will false religion misrepresent Jehovah and serve as a divisive influence on human society. No longer will servants of the true God experience injustice and exploitation at the hands of human authorities. What marvelous freedom will be enjoyed!

12 As "the Lamb of God that takes away the sin of the world," Jesus will apply the value of his sacrifice to cancel out the sins of mankind. (John 1:29) When Jesus was on earth and forgave a person's sins, he healed the forgiven one as proof of it. (Matthew 9:1-7; 15:30, 31) In like manner, Christ Jesus, as heavenly King of God's Kingdom, will miraculously heal the blind, the speechless, the deaf, the physically maimed, the mentally afflicted, and those with any other sickness. (Revelation 21:3, 4) All obedient ones will get "sin's law"

---

11. What marvelous freedom will be enjoyed by survivors of the great tribulation?
12. How will all be freed from sin and its effects?

nullified so that their thoughts and actions will be pleasing, both to themselves and to God. (Romans 7: 21-23) By the end of the Millennium, they will have been brought to human perfection, in the 'image and likeness' of the only true God.—Genesis 1:26.

13 When Christ has brought mankind to perfection, he will then give back to the Father the authority that was conferred upon him for this work: "He hands over the kingdom to his God and Father, when he has brought to nothing all government and all authority and power. For he must rule as king until God has put all enemies under his feet." (1 Corinthians 15:24, 25) The Millennial Rule of the Kingdom will have fully accomplished its purpose; so no longer will there be a need for this subsidiary government to remain between Jehovah and mankind. And since sin and death will have been completely removed and mankind redeemed, the need for Jesus as a Redeemer ends. The Bible explains: "Then the Son himself will also subject himself to the One who subjected all things to him, that God may be all things to everyone."—1 Corinthians 15:28.

14 Following this, perfected mankind will be given the opportunity to demonstrate that their choice is to serve the only true God forever. Hence, before fully adopting them as his children, Jehovah will subject all those perfected humans to a final test. Satan and his demons will be loosed from the abyss. This will result

---

13. At the end of the Millennial Rule, what action will Christ take, and with what result?
14. To what will all perfected humans be subjected, and why?

Obedient humans
will enjoy life in a
global paradise

in no lasting harm to those who truly love Jehovah. But any who disloyally allow themselves to be led into disobedience to Jehovah will be destroyed forever, along with the original rebel and his demons.—Revelation 20:7-10.

15 Jehovah will then adopt as his children all the perfected humans who upheld God's sovereignty during that final test. From that time on, they will share to the full the glorious freedom of the children of God as part of God's universal family. All intelligent creation in heaven and on earth will once again be united in worshiping him as the only true God. Jehovah's purpose will have attained glorious success! Do you want to be part of that happy, everlasting, universal family? If so, we encourage you to take to heart what the Bible says at 1 John 2:17: "The world is passing away and so is its desire, but he that does the will of God remains forever."

---

15. What situation will once again exist among all of Jehovah's intelligent creation?

Review Discussion

- Before the rebellion in Eden, what relationship did all worshipers of Jehovah have with him?
- What responsibility rests on those who are God's servants?
- Who will yet become children of God, and how is this related to Jehovah's purpose regarding united worship?

Would you welcome more information?

Write Jehovah's Witnesses at the appropriate address below.

ALASKA 99507: 2552 East 48th Ave., Anchorage. **ALBANIA:** Kutia postare 118, Tiranë. **ANGOLA:** Caixa Postal 6877, Luanda. **ARGENTINA:** Casilla de Correo 83 (Suc. 27B), 1427 Buenos Aires. **AUSTRALIA:** Box 280, Ingleburn, NSW 1890. **AUSTRIA (also Bulgaria, Macedonia, Yugoslavia):** Postfach 67, A-1134 Vienna. **BAHAMAS:** Box N-1247, Nassau, N.P. **BARBADOS, W.I.:** Crusher Site Road, Prospect, St. James. **BELGIUM:** rue d'Argile-Potaardestraat 60, B-1950 Kraainem. **BENIN, REP. OF:** 06 B.P. 1131, Akpakpa pk3, Cotonou. **BOLIVIA:** Casilla 6397, Santa Cruz. **BRAZIL:** Caixa Postal 92, 18270-970 Tatuí, SP. **BRITAIN:** The Ridgeway, London NW7 1RN. **CAMEROON:** B.P. 889, Douala. **CANADA:** Box 4100, Halton Hills (Georgetown), Ontario L7G 4Y4. **CENTRAL AFRICAN REPUBLIC:** B.P. 662, Bangui. **CHILE:** Casilla 267, Puente Alto. **COLOMBIA:** Apartado Postal 85058, Bogotá 8, D.C. **CONGO, DEMOCRATIC REPUBLIC OF:** B.P. 634, Limete, Kinshasa. **COSTA RICA:** Apartado 187-3006, Barreal, Heredia. **CÔTE D'IVOIRE (IVORY COAST), WEST AFRICA:** 06 B P 393, Abidjan 06. **CROATIA:** p.p. 58, HR-10090 Zagreb-Susedgrad. **CURAÇAO, NETHERLANDS ANTILLES:** P.O. Box 4708, Willemstad. **CYPRUS:** P.O. Box 11033, CY-2550 Dali. **CZECH REPUBLIC:** P.O. Box 90, 198 21 Prague 9. **DENMARK:** Stenhusvej 28, DK-4300 Holbæk. **DOMINICAN REPUBLIC:** Apartado 1742, Santo Domingo. **ECUADOR:** Casilla 09-01-1334, Guayaquil. **EL SALVADOR:** Apartado Postal 401, San Salvador. **ESTONIA:** Postbox 1075, 10302 Tallinn. **ETHIOPIA:** P.O. Box 5522, Addis Ababa. **FIJI:** Box 23, Suva. **FINLAND (also Latvia, Lithuania):** Postbox 68, FIN-01301 Vantaa. **FRANCE:** B.P. 625, F-27406 Louviers cedex. **GERMANY:** Niederselters, Am Steinfels, D-65618 Selters. **GHANA:** P. O. Box GP 760, Accra. **GREECE:** 77 Kifisias Ave., GR-151 24, Marousi, Athens. **GUADELOUPE:** Monmain, 97180 Sainte Anne. **GUATEMALA:** Apartado postal 711, 01901 Guatemala. **GUYANA:** 50 Brickdam, Georgetown 16. **GUYANE FRANÇAISE (FRENCH GUIANA):** 328 CD2, Route du Tigre, 97300 Cayenne. **HAITI:** Post Box 185, Port-au-Prince. **HAWAII 96819:** 2055 Kam IV Rd., Honolulu. **HONDURAS:** Apartado 147, Tegucigalpa. **HONG KONG:** 4 Kent Road, Kowloon Tong. **HUNGARY:** Cserkút u. 13, H-1162 Budapest. **INDIA:** Post Bag 10, Lonavla, Pune Dis., Mah. 410 401. **INDONESIA:** P.O. Box 2105, Jakarta 10001. **IRELAND:** Newcastle, Greystones, Co. Wicklow. **ITALY (also Israel):** Via della Bufalotta 1281, I-00138 Rome RM. **JAMAICA:** P. O. Box 103, Old Harbour, St. Catherine. **JAPAN:** 1271 Nakashinden, Ebina City, Kanagawa Pref., 243-0496. **KENYA:** P. O. Box 47788, 00100 Nairobi GPO. **KOREA, REPUBLIC OF:** Box 33 Pyungtaek P. O., Kyunggido, 450-600. **LIBERIA:** P. O. Box 10-0380, 1000 Monrovia 10. **LUXEMBOURG:** B. P. 2186, L-1021 Luxembourg, G. D. **MADAGASCAR:** B.P. 116, 105 Ivato. **MALAWI:** Box 30749, Lilongwe 3. **MALAYSIA:** Peti Surat No. 580, 75760 Melaka. **MARTINIQUE:** 20, rue de la Cour Campêche, 97200 Fort de France. **MAURITIUS:** Rue Baissac, Petit Verger, Pointe aux Sables. **MEXICO (also Belize):** Apartado Postal 896, 06002 Mexico, D. F. **MOZAMBIQUE:** Caixa Postal 2600, Maputo. **MYANMAR:** P.O. Box 62, Yangon. **NETHERLANDS:** Noordbargerstraat 77, NL-7812 AA Emmen. **NEW CALEDONIA:** BP 1741, 98874 Mont Dore. **NEW ZEALAND:** P O Box 75-142, Manurewa. **NICARAGUA:** Apartado 3587, Managua. **NIGERIA:** P.M.B. 1090, Benin City 300001, Edo State. **NORWAY:** Gaupeveien 24, N-1914 Ytre Enebakk. **PANAMA:** Apartado 6-2671, Zona 6A, El Dorado. **PAPUA NEW GUINEA:** P. O. Box 636, Boroko, NCD 111. **PARAGUAY:** Casilla de Correo 482, 1209 Asunción. **PERU:** Apartado 18-1055, Lima 18. **PHILIPPINES, REPUBLIC OF:** P. O. Box 2044, 1060 Manila. **POLAND:** Skr. Poczt. 13, PL-05-830 Nadarzyn. **PORTUGAL:** Apartado 91, P-2766-955 Estoril. **PUERTO RICO 00970:** P.O. Box 3980, Guaynabo. **ROMANIA (also Moldova):** Căsuţa Poştală nr. 132, O.P. 39 Bucureşti. **RUSSIA (also Belarus, Georgia, Kazakhstan):** ul. Srednyaya 6, p. Solnechnoye, 197739 St. Petersburg. **RWANDA:** B.P. 529, Kigali. **SLOVAKIA:** P.O. Box 17, 810 00 Bratislava 1. **SLOVENIA:** Poljanska cesta 77 A, p.p. 2019, SI-1001 Ljubljana. **SOLOMON ISLANDS:** P.O. Box 166, Honiara. **SOUTH AFRICA:** Private Bag X2067, Krugersdorp, 1740. **SPAIN:** Apartado 132, 28850 Torrejón de Ardoz (Madrid). **SRI LANKA, REP. OF:** 711 Station Road, Wattala 11300. **SURINAME:** P.O. Box 2914, Paramaribo. **SWEDEN:** Box 5, SE-732 21 Arboga. **SWITZERLAND:** P.O. Box 225, CH-3602 Thun. **TAHITI:** B.P. 7715, 98719 Taravao. **TAIWAN 327:** 3-12, Lin 7, Shetze Village, Hsinwu. **TANZANIA:** Box 7992, Dar es Salaam. **THAILAND:** 69/1 Soi Phasuk, Sukhumwit Rd., Soi 2, Bangkok 10110. **TOGO, WEST AFRICA:** B.P. 2983, Lomé. **TRINIDAD AND TOBAGO, REP. OF:** Lower Rapsey Street & Laxmi Lane, Curepe. **UKRAINE:** P.O. Box 246, 79000 Lviv. **UNITED STATES OF AMERICA:** 25 Columbia Heights, Brooklyn, NY 11201-2483. **URUGUAY:** Casilla 17030, 12500 Montevideo. **VENEZUELA:** Apartado 20.364, Caracas, DF 1020A. **ZAMBIA:** Box 33459, Lusaka 10101. **ZIMBABWE:** Private Bag WG-5001, Westgate.

Contact your local office for addresses in the following countries: Antigua, Guam, Iceland, Senegal, Sierra Leone.